FABRICE
MUAMBA
I'M STILL STANDING

FABRICE

MUAMBA

I'M STILL STANDING

MY INCREDIBLE STORY

Sport Media

To the heroes of my life.
You know who you are.

FABRICE
MUAMBA

Sport Media

By Fabrice Muamba with Chris Brereton

Copyright: Fabrice Muamba

Cover design: Rick Cooke
Cover image: Tony Woolliscroft

Published by Trinity Mirror Sport Media
Executive Editor: Ken Rogers
Senior Editor: Steve Hanrahan
Editor: Paul Dove
Senior Art Editor: Rick Cooke
Production: Alan Jewell, James Cleary
Design: Alison Barkley, Graeme Helliwell

First Edition
Published in Great Britain in 2012.
Published and produced by: Trinity Mirror Sport Media,
PO Box 48, Old Hall Street, Liverpool L69 3EB.

ISBN: 978-1-908695-40-6

Photography: Fabrice Muamba personal collection,
Trinity Mirror, PA Photos. Back page image: PA Photos

Printed and bound by CPI Group (UK) Ltd, Croydon, CR0 4YY

Contents

Acknowledgements

Thank You

THANK YOU. Two small words that make all the difference. And two words that will never do justice to the many people who have made sure that I'm still here, alive and well today.

First and foremost I'd like to thank God for giving me health, happiness and family and for also making sure I received the specialist care I needed to save my life.

Throughout my existence there have been a lot of challenges and a few ups and downs but at the end of all the adversity I've come out stronger than ever.

I couldn't have written this book by myself and I'd like to thank the people that have helped make it become a reality. My wife, Shauna Muamba, is the first on that list because she has been there for me from the moment we met. She's stood by me through thick and thin and she has given me a wonderful son, Joshua Jeremiah Muamba, who is not only my twin but also the love of my life. My love for these two people knows no boundaries and I'm glad I came back to grow older and wiser with them. I'd also like to thank my dad Marcel, mum Christine, step-mum Gertrude, Uncle Paul, Aunty Fifi, Hugo and my mother-in-law Marva Lashley for taking care of Joshua throughout that trying time back in March.

Eddie Kadi, Henri Bruno, Rashid Kamara, Johan Djourou (my brother from another mother), Thierry Henry aka Dikembe, David Bucho, Ike, Dr Mohiddin, Dr Deaner, Professor Schilling, Dr Tobin, all the doctors from Tottenham Hotspur, all the paramedics and ambulance staff, plus everybody who helped me at the London Chest Hospital and St Barts Hospital, also deserve a mention.

This entire book is a tribute to the amazing work that goes on in hospitals across the country every single day. I remain amazed by just how brilliant you all are. God has put all these people in my life for a reason and I love them and thank them from the bottom of my heart.

Football has been a huge part of my life and I've had the privilege to play with some of the best players in the world. I would like to thank Arsene Wenger for giving me the opportunity to play professional football with Arsenal and all the members of the club who encouraged and supported me.

Also, anyone connected to football – whether I trained with you, had a massage from you or just spoke with you – thank you for the experiences gained, they all collectively helped me become a better player and a better human being.

Bolton Wanderers is my club and they have been so supportive of me in my time of need especially the chairman Phil Gartside, owner of the football club Eddie Davies, Owen Coyle and the management team and staff that were employed at the club at the time.

Key Sports Management also deserve a mention as they've ensured that my career has progressed over the years. My agent Warwick Horton is someone I'm forever indebted to for all that he's done for me, for his advice, guidance and for managing every situation brilliantly.

Lastly I have to mention Chris Brereton who spent many hours with me not only writing this book but getting to know my family and I. Thank you for writing my story the way I wanted it to be told.

God has blessed me and helped me in so many ways. I thank every person who prayed for me when my situation seemed to be so hopeless.

Life is a precious thing – one moment you're up, one moment you're down, but in spite of all this remember God loves you and he will never leave you even in times of trouble. It's part of his master plan so just have faith.

Be inspired by this book, focus on your goals and you can achieve anything. God bless you all.

Fabrice Muamba, October, 2012

WHEN Fabrice died, I was sipping a pint in a Bangkok bar.

At the time I was working on the sports desk at the *Bangkok Post* newspaper and I, like everybody else, was desperate for information, desperate to know what had happened and what would happen. I went to bed that night fully expecting to read his obituary by the morning. It stayed that way for what felt like months.

From a professional point of view it was grim – deaths belong at the front of a newspaper not the back – and personally it was also a strange time. I was no different to the rest of the world, in journalism and elsewhere, who were hoping this young man would recover.

As time went on and Fabrice improved, I got the opportunity to return to the UK for a position with Trinity Mirror Sport Media.

I started the same week Fabrice announced his retirement.

In the middle of August – on my third day with the company and fifth day in the country – Steve Hanrahan, my senior editor, walked over and asked me a ridiculous question.

"Have you ever written an autobiography in six weeks?"

"No," was the obvious and accurate response.

I was told that talks had started with Fabrice and that I might be involved in some way. But writing a book in six weeks? From start to finish? That's impossible.

We did it in five.

Trust me, Fabrice isn't the only one scratching his head wondering about the twists and turns that life can take...

He is a tremendous guy. Everything you've already heard about him already is 100 per cent accurate. Humble, intelligent, polite, quiet and funny – he is the complete opposite of what you consider to be the average Premier League footballer. He is a man who clearly enjoys life, even more so now for obvious reasons, and he is hugely devoted to Shauna and Joshua, who are equally as passionate and caring about him in return.

Fabrice's life was an incredible tale before White Hart Lane even happened and helping him, in however small a role, since that time has been a pleasure, an honour and a great experience.

He is the first person I need to thank but certainly not the last.

Firstly, the entire team at Sport Media have been incredible in ensuring this book exists. The strict deadlines, which often threatened to send my head into an eternal spin, were managed beautifully by this brilliant and experienced crew.

Without wishing to pick out too many individuals, Ken Rogers, Will Beedles and, especially, Paul Dove and the aforementioned Steve have poured their time and expertise into what you are about to read. This book just wouldn't be here without them. It's as simple as that and to witness the way they've helped turn the raw product into the finished article is something I remain in awe of.

Jonathan Northcroft, Greg O'Keeffe, Robin Brown and Rory Smith also warrant a mention for the frequent times I've needed advice, a set of fresh eyes or both. They are all fine journalists and good friends. All the above helped keep me on track, as did Mark Boyns, who read the draft and chipped in with new ideas and suggestions.

Additionally, Dr Tobin, Owen Coyle, Phil Mason and Mark Alderton at Bolton Wanderers, Dr Deaner, Dr Mohiddin, Professor Schilling, Angela Boon and Hayley Burwell at Barts Health NHS Trust and Peter Fisher and Alistair Drummond from the London Ambulance Service have all been supportive in helping me fill in the gaps of what happened on that day back in March. Many thanks to them all. I must also applaud Arsenal's Steve Leonard and Dan Tolhurst for all their assistance in talking me through Fabrice's time at the club.

Fabrice's wife, Shauna, has also been a wonderful help and someone who deserves a huge amount of thanks and recognition.

As this book shows, the role she played in Fabrice's recovery was so important and her strength, then and now, is a lesson to us all.

Lastly, and most importantly, I want to praise my family for all that they are and all they have been. When you spend many hours interviewing a young man about what dying does to your perspective on life, it cannot help but make you consider your own thoughts on what counts. In my case it has just confirmed what I've always known to be true: I'm the luckiest man alive, including Fabrice himself.

I will never be able to truly express my gratitude for the wonderful start to life that I've had and the unconditional love and support received from my mum Mary, dad Steve, sister Cassie plus all four of my grandparents, all of whom I've been lucky enough to know and grow up around. It's been a blast. May it long continue.

Chris Brereton, October, 2012

Introduction

My Life Story

I KNOW why you're reading this. Don't worry, I'd be doing the same if I was you.

In the same way that the motorway is jammed for miles and miles when there is a crash, and everybody slows down to take a look when they pass the scene, I know that my collapse and everything that followed was pretty strange and unique. It's only natural to want to know more when something shocking happens. It's human nature.

Yet when there is a crash on the motorway only a few people really see it. When I died, everybody was watching – the match was broadcast on television and the instant media reaction meant my story went around the world before I was even stretchered off. As a result I have no issue at all with people knowing who I am and being interested in my life solely because of those crazy moments at White Hart Lane. People were shocked and stunned by what happened. They weren't the only ones.

I'd always intended on writing a book because I felt that my life story was far more interesting than most professional footballers'. I won't lie and claim that I planned on sorting one out in these circumstances or quite so soon. I fancied a decent read about 15 years from now where you would read the Fabrice Muamba story on the back of a career full of England caps and silverware. However, life had other things in store for me.

I never dreamt, not in a million years, that I would be the centre of a story like this. I shouldn't really be here. I cannot believe I'm still here. God has his own plans for each and every one of us but it's still hard to understand what I've been through.

How does a fit 23-year-old Premier League footballer, who has never had any previous health scares or career-threatening injuries, end up face down and dying in front of thousands of people in a stadium? Then, unbelievably, why does his heart start working 78 minutes later? How can he be lucky enough to have some of the country's best medics working on him within seconds of collapsing?

Why did this happen to me?

How did I survive?

How did I come back?

The questions go on and on and on but I don't mind any of them. I also have no problem in people mentioning the "D" word either. Some think I will be offended if they ask me whether I believe I actually died or not.

In my eyes, I was dead. Beyond hope. Gone.

The medical world might see it slightly differently, claiming instead that I just stopped breathing and had no heart output, but if that isn't a definition of "dead", then I don't know what is! That is dead in my book – the one you're reading now – and I want to make that as clear as can be.

When I woke up on that cold March morning, even in my wildest imagination I would never have been able to foresee the amazing chain of events that would unfold. That my life would pretty much end... but yet I would still survive.

And, of course, my story isn't finished there.

Coming back was just the start for me. The road to recovery would be a long and winding one. Adapting to a new future, with targets to strive for, potential pitfalls to avoid and obstacles to overcome, wouldn't always be easy. I came to realise that the life I formerly knew would change forever. I had to find the courage to change with it, the inner strength to believe that I could be a new Fabrice Muamba. The same, only different. Reborn.

But I'm still here. I'm still standing.

#1

Judgement Day

MARCH 17, 2012. This is it. This is my chance. The drizzle falls from the skies as we emerge from the tunnel. The thrill of match-day. The sense of expectation. Everything I've ever wanted, it's all here in this moment. The chance to show what I can do, to be a professional footballer.

We walk out in our team lines. Bolton in black, Spurs in white. The fans rise from their seats and clap, songs echo out from pockets in the stands. This is it. Under the lights and on Saturday night television. The cameras follow our every move as we step on to the pitch that is crisp and moist with the rain, perfect for passing.

I glance up at the big screen that is built into the stand at one end of the ground. A full house at White Hart Lane.

We are one game from Wembley. It will be tough, no doubt about it. It's a hard draw but we're in the last eight of the Cup, the FA Cup. The trophy that every boy who loves football dreams of winning.

The week leading up to the game has been the same as any other. I am feeling really great, just the usual Fabrice. An easy going and normal guy who gets on with his job. If anyone wants anything doing – for the team or for a mate or whoever – then I'll happily get on with it and do it. I don't think there's anything special about me.

But I'll be honest. The season hasn't been easy. Not everything has gone according to plan, not for me or Bolton. We've struggled for results and I haven't been a regular in the side. I've been in and out of the starting line-up, which is frustrating. My last start was against Chelsea at Stamford Bridge on February 25 and they taught us a lesson, beating us 3-0. After that, I sat on the bench for the defeat to Manchester City a week later before again coming on as a substitute when we beat QPR. No player wants to be dropped and I'm the same. The Spurs game is a chance, my chance, to get back into the team and keep my place.

So I'm looking forward to the trip. The FA Cup will be a welcome break from the league, and a chance to dream of playing at Wembley again. It's a special place and a special competition. Don't believe the doubters who say the FA Cup is not what it was. There is no better feeling than playing at Wembley.

Sometimes you get an idea of what the team selection will be well before the weekend and on the Thursday before the game there is a huge hint that the gaffer Owen Coyle will be making changes from the side that has just beaten QPR. My hopes are up that I will be getting the nod. Without anything official being said, Coyle makes it clear that I'm in. In my head I start to prepare myself for the game. I'm feeling physically sharp and mentally fine.

I go home after training and follow the usual routine. I pray for God to give me the confidence to play and do well. I speak to my dad, Marcel, and we agree that we will speak again in the morning. As far as I'm concerned, everything is looking great. I have nothing to worry about, nothing to be stressed about, nothing to fear.

That night, I pack my bag for the trip to London. Before an away game on a Saturday I always sort my travel stuff on a Thursday night. I can't be bothered doing it on a Friday as it's usually a full and busy day. It's much better if it's ready before we set off for wherever we are playing. One less thing to have on your mind ahead of a game. I spend the rest of the evening getting prepared before another typical 'me' night – relaxed, chilled, stress-free.

#####

I get up on Friday and follow my usual routine. Nothing out of the ordinary. I have my Crunchy Nut Cornflakes, pray with my partner, Shauna, and set off for the training ground where I can prepare for the game.

I do have another role on away journeys – I'm the chief food organiser. Shauna has her own catering service and some of the boys order from her on a regular basis. And for a good reason. I might be biased but her cooking is amazing. The boys ring her up, get her to cook them some of her Caribbean classics – her jerk chicken is the best in the world – and then it's my job to take it with me so the boys can enjoy it on the train. Chicken, rice and peas, plantain – they will eat anything they can get their hands on. You should see them. They absolutely love it. On that Friday, Zat Knight, Darren Pratley, Nigel Reo-Coker, Ivan Klasnic and me all had enough to keep us going on the journey. When they're eating Shauna's magic it's the only time they're quiet. You can ask anyone from Rio Ferdinand to Emile Heskey – they all get their food from Shauna.

So after getting home from training I pick up the food orders and get a lift to Stockport station from Shauna.

I'm feeling good. Nothing is wrong. All is well. Just another Friday before matchday. Getting myself ready. Preparing. Making sure I'm in the right frame of mind, all set to do what I do best: play football, live my dream.

We get to Euston at about 4pm after our usual journey. A couple of hours full of chat, banter, card playing and ribbing. It's the same in any football club all over the world. We're having a laugh and a joke because life is good. We're on our way to play a game of football, so how can we not be happy?

I sit with Ivan Klasnic. He's a good guy. He is such a character and he is very... how shall I put this? Very German! He says what he thinks and he says it up front. I like that. I see a different side to him than most in football, so I know him well. I have loads of mates in football and many of them are like Ivan – two different people; the guy on the pitch and the guy off it.

We just sit and relax before arriving at our hotel in Regent's Park in St John's Wood. Business as usual once more. On a

Friday, after our evening meal, the gaffer likes to get us all together for a chat about what lies ahead. Pasta and meatballs is on the menu – along with plenty of water – and that gives us the boost we need before a match, even if it doesn't come close to Shauna's efforts earlier in the day!

Owen gives a short presentation on what we need to do the following afternoon. We already know that Spurs are likely to be tough because they are so strong at home. Luka Modric and Scott Parker are playing brilliantly for them. The boss, Harry Redknapp, is doing a great job, their team spirit is clearly high and he has the right balance in his squad. He knows how to put the different pieces together.

It will be a difficult evening.

When I am mentally preparing for a game, however, I always concentrate on myself more than the opposition. The minute I start worrying and focusing on our opponents is the moment I lose focus and the moment I start giving the game away. My own match is all that matters – let the rest take care of itself. Push yourself, compose yourself, be the best you can be. That is what these talks from the gaffer are all about and that is what we are all trying to do.

After the meeting, Jhamal John, a London barber I know, comes round to cut my hair in my room. He's been a mate for about five years, he looks after people like Daniel Sturridge, Theo Walcott, Zat, Shaun Wright-Phillips and Johan Djourou and always does a good job. So much for the endless glamour of being a Premier League footballer. The night before a game can be as normal and as boring as getting your head trimmed.

After this is done, I speak to my dad and Shauna again and pray with them both, asking God for protection and safety. I'm so desperate to play well and I know God can help me.

> *'God, please let me perform to my best, let me and my team-mates prosper.'*

I just want to get out there and win and praying leads to playing, or at least I think it does. Afterwards I relax in my room and use the internet on my phone. Soon, sleep comes. I sleep really well, as always.

#####

Saturday morning and matchday is here at last. I wander down to breakfast at 9.30am and see the physio, Andy Mitchell, or 'Mitch' as we know him, club masseur Harry Brooke, who is a really great guy, and all the players. I sit with Martin Petrov and we discuss the TV from the night before, share a few laughs and just relax. By now I can't wait for the game to come but it's a 5.30pm kick-off and I have a few hours to kill. I decide not to go for a walk and go back to my room, waiting for the pre-match meal, saving mental energy, keeping my nerves in check. I make another quick phone call to my dad, who I've secured a match ticket for, and also Shauna.

We say our final prayers together before I have to leave the hotel. On the day of a game there is an itinerary to follow. What time you have to be in reception, ready to go and so on. Some people think all the players' doors are knocked on or that we have a chaperone to help us but that's rubbish. You have to take care of yourself and that is the way it should be.

I make sure I make it to reception on time before the gaffer starts handing out any fines. I pay £15 for the internet I've used in the room. Not the club. I pay for it myself. Like I say, it's good for you as a person if you have to take responsibility for things you have used. Why should footballers be any different?

Getting to White Hart Lane is no more eventful than any other journey to a ground. I sit near the back of the bus on my own, collecting my thoughts, refusing to get too excited too early, keeping myself to myself, working out how to be the best I can be.

After signing for a ticket for my dad, my brother Daniel and my 'cousin' Alvin – he's one of those cousins who's not actually related but is the son of one of your dad's best mates – I start to focus on what we need to do as a team. The dressing room is covered in plans and tactics. Plans for what we do when defending corners, plans for how to counter Redknapp's attacking play, plans for how to get out of London with a safe passage into the semi-finals of the FA Cup and another visit to Wembley.

The pitch looks in great condition so I decide to wear my studs rather than my moulded boots. I want my feet to be sharp and I prefer studs. These are the minor details that you piece together to give yourself half a chance when it's time to go to war. My white Nike Tiempo boots are ready.

As I walk around the pitch, I listen to my headphones and relax. On this day, I decide that gospel music is what I want to listen to. Everybody is different and feels the need to get hyped up in different ways. I prefer to stay nice and calm and gospel music allows me to do that. There are probably not many Premier League players who listen to gospel music but a lot of people lose their identity when they enter the football world. They seem to forget where they are from, who they are and what they stand for as an individual. I am a Christian so I need to represent Christ. I listen to rap as well and I enjoy it but gospel music just so happens to help me the most. I need music that is dedicated to God on this day. It is my choice.

White Hart Lane is practically empty at this point before we head back in to listen to the gaffer officially announce his starting XI. I am in there and I can't wait to get out and express myself. This is my reward for training hard and being patient. I'm determined to do well for the team and prove to the gaffer that I'm good enough to start every game. Every player uses that as a motivation and I'm no different. I want to keep the shirt for the next match. Once I have it, it's my possession to keep or lose – you can only give your shirt away, nobody can take it off you.

I'm waiting. I'm ready. Kick-off is coming.

I have to make the most of my chance. While I get my ankles strapped, in preparation for the battle ahead, Shauna is miles away, at home in Cheshire. She is having a long day. She's taken our son, Joshua, to a birthday party all afternoon and watched him run around like the fun-loving three-year-old he is. It's now time to watch daddy enjoying his Saturday as well.

All around me people begin getting massages while I start to feel super-focused and ready. The dressing room looks and smells no different to a Sunday League version, all ointments and sticky tape, noise and adrenaline.

With an hour to go before kick-off, the music begins as everyone starts trying to put their selections on the main speakers. We have a special match compilation that we play before the game, full of recent hits and tunes that will get us going. At least that keeps the arguments down over who gets to play what.

I don't want to get too excited. It's a balancing act. I want to stay as mellow as possible. I don't want to blow mental energy on something as stupid as the pre-match tunes. It's about staying level-headed and finding your peace of mind and getting ready for the warm-up. Boxer shorts first, then shorts, warm-up top, socks and boots. That is my method. There is no superstition involved in that, it's just the way I am as a person.

Our fitness coach, Jimmy Barrow, leads us in the warm-up, getting our muscles loose and warm, making us sprint over ladders and between cones, tightening our reactions and getting our brains in tune with our bodies.

Some people don't understand how important it is to stretch your mind as well as your body before a match. The two need to be working together if you want to start a game well. We get involved in small passing drills and I feel fine.

I still have no idea about what lies ahead. Nothing. I could never be prepared for what is about to happen to me.

We return to the dressing room for one final preparation just five minutes before kick-off. Everybody is dripping with sweat as the room starts steaming up. We all dry ourselves off before swapping our training tops for our matchday shirts, absorbing and listening to the gaffer's final words of advice as well as taking on board the experience of the senior players.

Kevin Davies has always been a brilliant leader and before this match he is no different, speaking his mind as he ties his boots, letting us know what he expects from Spurs and what he expects from us. Some teams love shouting before a match while others are more analytical, talking about keeping clean sheets and what each person has to do. No two dressing rooms are the same.

At Bolton everyone chips in when something needs to be said and the senior players lead by example. Zat, Nigel and Martin all keep us in a good frame of mind and get us ready for the game. Two minutes before we go out Owen has his final say before we head for the pitch. He wants us to defend well, stay positive and take our chances. Owen is a good man to play for and you can see how much he wants us to do ourselves justice.

In the tunnel, the mood switches into work mode. Now it's time to do my job. If I know someone on the other side I will shake their hand and check they are ok but nothing more than that. Mainly I'm a quiet person. I always prefer to say nothing unless I need to, especially just before the game. I want my football to talk for me.

The pre-game rituals pass with a blur. I'm not worried about anything at all. I'm ready. Let's get on with the action. This is it. This is my chance.

Howard Webb gets the game underway, I settle in nice and quickly before I try to take more control as my confidence grows.

Suddenly we're in the lead. Goal. Great start. Nelsen gets a touch to Ricketts' cross and puts off Walker, who concedes a corner. The ball is played to the near post and Pratley gets a head to the ball. It flicks off Bale's shoulder and beats Cudicini. 1-0. Just the start we wanted. The game starts again. There is no let-up. Both teams going toe to toe. I show quick feet in the middle of the pitch but Miyaichi can't force his way down the flank.

In the dugout, our club doctor Jonathan Tobin is having the time of his life. The 41-year-old, a huge Spurs fan, is sat at White Hart Lane watching the men he knows and respects medically facing the men he knows and admires personally.

He turns to Jimmy Barrow and mentions how fortunate he is. "Jimmy," he says, "can you believe we're getting paid for this? I'm at White Hart Lane, in the dugout watching my team. This is ridiculous. Does it get any better?"

How quickly life can change. How quickly life can end.

Then, another goal. An equaliser. Our early lead is gone in no time at all. Bale is full of power and pace, a constant threat down the left. He delivers a cross to the back post. Walker towers into the sky. Above Alonso. His header flashes past Bogdan. 1-1. We must fight, give everything tonight. Give everything for Wembley.

They have some really quick players and I know that when they counter-attack I have to get back as soon as possible. That is constantly on my mind.

If Bale gets past me I will have to bring him down if that's what it takes to stop him. That's life at the tough end of football. Sometimes you have to sacrifice yourself for the team. That's just the way the game is played. If that means a yellow or even a red card then I'll just have to take my medicine.

After about 25 minutes I get a slight tingly headache. It doesn't last more than two minutes and then I completely forget about it. There is no reason to be fearful or overly worried about it. The pace of this game is so quick, I have no time to think about anything other than the situation in front of me.

If you can ignore the crowd's chants and all the verbals launched at you at every away ground in the country, you can ignore something as minor as a headache. I shrug it off. I get on with the game.

Then, I have a chance. A minute after Petrov shoots wide, we come forward again. Petrov crosses but Miyaichi can't get to the ball. But we win a corner. Petrov takes it and all of a sudden I have an opportunity. The ball is fed in low to me. Just as I am about to let fly, I slip. The ball flies high into the stands. Chance gone. Spurs have let the pace drop a little. I push up as we build from right to left. Pratley gets inside the box and squares for me. I take a touch. There is no time. The space has gone.

Now I feel another headache. Different to the one before. It is stronger, much more painful.

There is nothing I can do to stop it. For the first time in my playing career I think I will need half-time pills to get me through. Either that or a new head.

My skull feels like it is being crushed, the right side is proper agony and my vision begins to play tricks on me. Now I'm standing in the middle of the pitch feeling very, very dizzy.

It hits home that this isn't something normal. My vision is going. Everything is blurred. Through the pain I begin to realise I have never had a headache like this before in my life.

I just want to get to the break and get myself sorted.

I hope Dr Tobin can give me something or spray me with something that will make it all go away. Before I can think further about getting any treatment, Bale is once again flying down the left wing.

I hear Zat calling my name, his frantic shouts of "COME BACK, COME BACK" breaking through the fog in my head.

As much as I want to sprint back my legs are refusing to listen. They know something I don't.

All of a sudden Spurs have got two Luka Modrics and two Scott Parkers.

What is happening to me?

A split second later my head smashes into the White Hart Lane turf. As it bounces once I am alive. By the time it bounces twice I am dead. I am gone. And the last words I had heard were "come back".

I couldn't have put it better myself.

#2

Living A Dream

I STAGGER home. I'm covered in sweat and dust and sporting the odd bruise or two. Again. Same old story. The ball's tucked under my arm and my schoolbag is flung over my shoulder, following behind me.

"Where have you been?" asks mum. She is angry.

"I've been out, playing football after school," I reply, as if she didn't know.

"What about your food? You haven't eaten again. This is no good Fabrice, this can't go on."

This is the childhood scene that would be replayed time and time again. As soon as I left school at midday, I would be off to find a game and I'd just ignore meal times and anything else mum said. Football was the only thing on my mind. I loved it. We didn't really have pitches, we used to just play on sand and gravel wherever we could find it. We didn't know anything else and we thought we were the luckiest kids alive. I went to Mokengeli Literary High School until lunchtime and would then go out with my mates, walking wherever we needed to try and find a game of football against anyone who wanted to take us on.

I'd be gone for hours, picking different boys up from different avenues along the way. The closest pitch to mine was about 20 minutes away but even calling it a pitch is a stretch because there were no markings or goalmouths. We just had to use our brains and we always kind of knew how far the ball could go before it went out of play. We didn't need goals because we just played for sheer fun. It wasn't scoring that mattered, it was about playing with your friends and being outside.

We used to play barefoot and mum would go crazy. My feet and legs would be badly cut all the time. Kicking the ball on stones and sand meant you couldn't avoid getting shredded ankles and toes.

"Stop doing that, I've told you," she would say. "Every day is the same." It was the only time I ever ignored her because I loved playing so much, I just loved the freedom and the laughter. Playing football made us all closer as friends.

In many ways, my upbringing was a typical African football story. We never actually played with a proper football. What we used to do was get a balloon, blow it up, wrap about 10 shopping bags and loads of rags around it to give it some weight and then tie it all together with strong laces to keep it all together. The older boys used to make it and I would sit there amazed at their skill.

They would be so patient, taking their time to try and get the shape of a proper ball. They would even tie the laces on top in such a way that it looked like the ball had real panels and patterns. I was taught how to do it but I was never that good so I used to leave it up to the others. Everyone in Congo did the same thing. The ball wouldn't be perfect but it was better than nothing. It would take a rough bounce here and there but that just added to the fun. When the rags and laces and everything else came undone we just made another one. Nothing was going to stop us playing.

I remember so well the first time I played with a proper football. Wow. I was 10 years old and a guy I knew had a brother who lived in Europe. He came back one day with a present – an Adidas Telstar! It's the ball that is designed with the black and white panels on it. It was love at first sight. Oh my God, I was so jealous.

My friend didn't want anyone to play with the ball, he wanted to keep it nice and fresh. But I couldn't keep quiet and soon told everyone that we could be playing with a real, proper, perfect ball.

He wouldn't bring it out but I just wouldn't shut up and in the end, he brought it with him to our pitch. I've never been so excited. Is this what the kids in Europe play with? Is this how lucky those guys are? Get me to Europe now! It was just so different. The smell, the way it moved, how easy it was to shoot and pass with. When you hit a straight pass it went straight, it didn't wobble to one side like our footballs did. The more he brought it the more we enjoyed it. Sometimes, he would only bring it on a Saturday. That meant the six other days of the week we went back to our own raggy ball, but that just made us appreciate it even more. We would count down the days until we played with the Telstar again.

I just couldn't get enough of football when I was young. When

France won the World Cup in 1998 I remember watching it and becoming obsessed with that team. Patrick Vieira, Zinedine Zidane, Thierry Henry, Robert Pires – wow. I remember one game where Henry was brilliant and I got out of bed the next day and I had an announcement for all my friends.

"I'm not Fabrice anymore – please don't call me that," I said. "Call me Henry." We were always doing stuff like that. Some of my mates would tell their mums to not call them by their names at all, demanding to be called Zidane or Pires or Anelka.

During the holidays I would be out of the door before seven in the morning and would get back at seven or eight at night. Mum knew she couldn't keep me in the house or around the place so would give me some money to get food while I was out.

We'd play and play and I'd use all my money on Fanta. I've never been a big eater so it all went on drinks with a bit of bread every now and then. Even now, when I taste Fanta it takes me back to those times and the great memories I had of being an innocent kid just kicking a ball – and maybe even a Telstar – about.

#####

The ball drifts behind our goalkeeper Adam Bogdan's net for a goal-kick. Bogdan waits. The ball passes from his right to his left hand as he weighs up the situation. He pats his chest and raises a gloved palm to a team-mate. Wait. The goal-kick will have to wait. Something is not right. His eyes focus upfield where I lie on the grass, eight yards from the halfway line.

Dead. For 78 minutes, I won't be here. How do I even begin to tell this story?

Bale jogs back and glances over to this shape on the floor. I'm face down on the turf. The floodlights illuminate the white number 6 on the back of my black top. The studs of my boots can be seen as I lie with my legs apart, just as I've fallen. My left arm is tucked underneath me, my right almost rooted in the turf. People start panicking big time.

#####

The opening chapters of my life made me the man I am today. They gave me the values I carry forward into every area of my life, they are my inspiration and so much of what I now do is based on what happened when I was young.

Although most people think I was born in Kinshasa in the Democratic Republic of Congo, I was actually born in Lubumbashi in the south-east of the country. When I was born, in April 1988, the country was still officially called Zaire. It would change its name in 1997 following a nightmare time that would leave me and my family scared for our lives.

When people think of Africa and Africans many believe life is just one long, tough grind. There is always a ten-mile walk for water, or huge famine or poverty. That is how the story goes. While that is true for far too many people, there are also families who live normal, happy and prosperous lives. And we were definitely one of those.

Along with my mum, Christine, and dad, Marcel, I can honestly say that the early years of my life in Congo were as risk-free, relaxed and as enjoyable as living anywhere else on the planet.

We moved to Kinshasa when I was two because of dad's work. Kinshasa is the capital of Congo and back then it was ok. It wasn't anything like Europe but it was where I belonged and learned so much. It was a place that allowed me to spend time with my family and friends, a place where I could grow up – and play endless games of football – in peace and happiness. Or so we all thought.

We lived in a big house in a nice neighbourhood. It was a one-level property but there were about five bedrooms. It was spacious and an enjoyable place to live. The weather was usually nice and hot, it didn't rain too much and I was like any young African boy – obsessed with the outdoors and sport.

I absolutely loved school. So many kids went to it that the day was split into two – the early pupils and the afternoon pupils. I would go until midday before the other set of kids arrived for lessons between 1pm and 5pm. It was a long day for the teachers but the place was wonderful, if a little scary at times.

Unlike England where kids attend school from a really young age, I didn't start going until much later. I was either seven or eight when I began formal education and that allowed me to play and to learn about life and to spend time with my family. Rather than being in a classroom from the age of five onwards, I was with my family and that was so important.

I was a decent kid and just tried to keep my head down. It was completely different to school in the UK. The teachers were so strict. If you didn't do your homework, it was time to prepare for a full-blown rant. In England you get the chance to say "sorry Miss, I forgot it" but if you tried to pull that stunt in Congo then the teachers would tear into you in no time at all. And if you skipped school then not even God himself could save you.

That was just the African mentality – work hard, be disciplined, do your classes and your homework. If you didn't do them or you were stupid enough to ignore a teacher or show them disrespect then they would bring your whole world crashing down and it wasn't pretty. Who wants to spend all night doing homework anyway? Get it done quickly and then go and kick a football around with your mates. That was my thinking anyway.

My teachers gave me the discipline and drive needed to help me improve while respecting my elders and being faithful to God. I mainly studied Maths, Geography and French. I spoke Lingala at home and I could've chosen to learn English but I picked French instead – what a life-changing decision that would turn out to be...

Mine was a fee-paying school and I was brought up knowing that it was a privilege to go to such a great place. It was a wonderful experience and it allowed me to study hard. It sorted out the building blocks of my life. Not every kid can go to a good school – it's no different than England in that way.

Everybody called me by my nickname Fala. Everyone knew me, everyone knew Fala, the guy who likes to smile. I liked getting on with everyone, I would try and mix with my whole school. I didn't need a best friend, we all just got on. In Congo, if your dad worked for the government like mine did, some kids would carry themselves like they were something but not me.

There was only one person I respected and feared more than the teachers and that was dad. Thank God I never got into trouble in the classroom! If news got back home that I wasn't doing my homework or had been disrespectful to an elder I think I would have run away. I would have been too scared to go through my own front door.

Dad is quite tall and a big broad, stocky man. He is very quiet but when he says something it stays said. He speaks his mind while being laid back at the same time. I love and admire him massively. He was and is a wonderful father but he was also a strict disciplinarian.

It is an African way to show your mother and father respect and to conduct yourself in the right manner. I used to get the odd clip around the ear if I did step out of line but generally when dad said something he only had to say it once.

With dad being away most of the time with work, me and mum formed a special bond. Mum is down to earth, mellow and relaxed. She knows how to speak to everybody. Mums run the house all over the world and mine is the same. She is the boss lady – a woman with a kind heart. It was great to feel so much love coming from one person. Yes she was a tough, strong woman but her love was there for everyone to see and I felt it from such an early age.

I was an only child but there were so many family members coming in and out I didn't really notice that. Our house was always open and there was never a day when it was quiet and dull. I really liked that although sometimes a bit of peace would have been nice! But it's better to have too much love and too much family rather than none at all.

My early childhood was full of laughter and love. You can't ask for any more. Growing up in Kinshasa was interesting, varied, full of sunshine and laughter. One of my early memories is of me sitting in the kitchen watching mum prepare rice and peas – the African way of cooking them both separately before combining them – and thinking how lucky I was to be going to a good school with two parents who loved me. Not everyone gets that. Maybe I was living a dream and, as with all dreams, that would have to end at some point. And it did when dad, the most influential man in my young life, suddenly had to leave the country overnight.

#####

'GET ON THE PITCH! GET ON THE PITCH! GET ON THE PITCH!'

Andy Mitchell, our physio, has arrived from nowhere and is screaming down his microphone to Dr Tobin. All thoughts of a wonderful White Hart Lane adventure are forgotten. Mitch has been looking in my direction as I fall.

He knows straight away. The way I don't try to stop myself from butting the turf is all the evidence he needs to see that this is a bad one.

Forget waiting for referee Howard Webb to give consent, Mitch is up and running in no time at all. He is kneeling over me, his head close to mine, inspecting me, looking for signs of consciousness. Something is not right.

This is no ordinary injury. The orange stripes on the boots of Nigel Reo-Coker, are inches from my face as he stands over me, hands on hips, concerned. Spurs' Rafael van der Vaart, William Gallas and Louis Saha are there as well.

Peter Fisher, a London Ambulance Service-trained paramedic, is a Spurs fan like Dr Tobin.

He spends matchdays working for X9 Services, a private ambulance company who provide on-field medical care when Spurs are at home. During the week he works for the London Ambulance Service full-time and they also have their own staff at the ground today. Everyone knows Peter. He's part of the furniture.

He's never been needed for anything serious in his five years on the White Hart Lane sidelines.

Not yet...

He sits to the left of the Spurs dugout. Close enough to see the polish on Harry Redknapp's shoes, close enough to hear Joe Jordan shouting instructions.

Close enough to see me collapse.

As I lie on the ground, Wayne Diesel, Spurs' head of medical services, also knows exactly what he is seeing.

"Pete, get on," he shouts before Peter utters the words he never thought his brain would form or his mouth would speak.

"He's dead Wayne," he responds, racing out of his seat, picking up the stretcher with the help of his X9 colleagues.

"That boy is dead."

#3

Leaving

SHAUNA is more than happy to keep Joshua occupied with the
TV. She knows how important this match against Tottenham is,
how much I want to use the FA Cup to prove to the gaffer that I
deserve a place in his Premier League plans after being dropped.
She loves watching me play apart from the tackling. She hates
how I fly in and thinks I'm going to injure myself.

It's a late kick-off but that's not the end of the world. Shauna
sits in her pyjamas, as does Joshua, and thinks about cooking me
salmon and pasta when I arrive back home later this evening.

It's a horrible night and she's settled in and has no plans to go
anywhere. She sips her tea and nibbles on a slice of toast. As she
brushes the crumbs off her lap she takes her eyes off the telly.
When she looks up she sees me lying on the grass. That slice of

toast is the last thing she will eat for three days.

On the pitch, Mitch continues checking me. This is definitely no ordinary injury. He reaches under my midriff and attempts to lift me over, to perform a 'log-roll' procedure. I can't be turned. He tries again, and Reo-Coker attempts to help. It is not easy, I am unresponsive.

About 120 miles away, my agent Warwick Horton is on the couch at home. He's knackered. He's been watching Aston Villa Under-18s play Crystal Palace earlier today and isn't in the mood for the comedy club night he is heading for with his wife, Suzanne, in Birmingham city centre. He kicks his shoes off and just wants to watch the match, ignoring the calls from upstairs to have a shower and get ready. He convinces his wife to let him see the game until half-time so he can see how I'm doing. Plus the couch is comfortable. Not for long.

"Suzanne," he shouts. "Come downstairs."

"Why?" comes the response.

"Just come down here quickly," Warwick replies.

And she does. And she bursts into tears on the spot.

#####

Before I could even point to where England was on a world map, I'd already lived a life that was perfect for a novel. It read like a spy thriller.

President Mobutu had been the leader of Zaire since 1965 and was responsible for bringing Muhammad Ali and George Foreman to the country for the 'Rumble in the Jungle' classic in 1974. He was a president who still divides opinion and who eventually had to flee the country himself in 1997 as he became hunted by rebel forces. He was also the man that dad called 'Boss'.

Dad was an adviser to the president and was one of his most trusted helpers. He travelled with him everywhere. I knew dad must have been important as he went to work in a suit while all my uncles went to work in just a shirt. I remember noticing that and thinking 'my dad must do something different'. There was no doubt about that. One of the reasons I could afford to go to a good school was because dad was well paid by the government.

When I was about seven we began to hear about trouble in the east of Congo. There was always trouble in nearby Rwanda and it started to spill over the border. But what did that mean to a tiny boy obsessed with football? It didn't really bother me and my parents didn't seem too worried about it either. That would soon change. Life in Kinshasa was safe and enjoyable and we expected it all to settle down and the trouble to go away. In fact, it had only just started.

Dad's links to the president would eventually leave me without a father for five years and would leave me and mum in a state of constant worry and fear.

By the mid-1990s, President Mobutu was a deeply unpopular man in parts of the country and that led to the rise of a man called Laurent-Désiré Kabila who had plans to take control. I don't know too much of the detail but I do know that when the new regime was trying to get power they were targeting everyone around the president.

That meant that my dad was in serious danger.

Kabila wanted President Mobutu dead and he managed to get loads of different politicians and mini-armies to unite and target the president. Marcel Muamba's name was also on the wanted list.

If he hung around he was a dead man.

It was a bit like a football team really. When a manager is sacked and a new regime comes in, all of his old supporters are sacked with him. The only difference in this case is that dad would've been killed. That is Africa for you.

I remember the day he left so clearly. Losing your dad is hardly something you're going to forget in a hurry, is it? It was a bright Sunday afternoon and he just said "I'll see you soon." That was it. I had no idea he was fleeing the country, going for good, saving his own life.

I thought he was just going away on business as usual. There were no tears from him or me. Why would I cry? I thought he'd be back soon, the same as always.

Mum didn't say anything either. After five or six days, however, I realised that this wasn't normal. "Why hasn't he come back?" I asked mum, sensing that I was about to hear bad news.

"Your dad's in danger," she said. "He has had to go to another country."

Can you imagine the confusion that caused? I was so young and naïve and didn't know what she meant. Mum tried to explain the situation and told me that people wanted to take over from the president. Nothing really sunk in. I couldn't work out why dad had left.

Dad's exit also meant the end of my parents' relationship. Mum and dad had grown apart due to the pressure they were under and that meant that when dad left his son on that day, he also left his marriage.

I say 'marriage' but in fact, I don't think there is an official form of marriage in Congo. There is no regulation or paperwork. Mum wore a ring and they were together but there was no formal divorce because there was no formal marriage in the first place.

Some children go mad when their parents split up but mum wouldn't allow that. She made me go to school, she forced me to be brave and to try and forget dad's departure. I suppose, looking back, she was trying to protect me from the harsh truth that both our lives were now in massive danger too.

We were on the verge of death.

It wouldn't have taken five minutes for the new regime to trace dad's footsteps back to us and then who knows what could have happened? We lived in constant fear.

At any moment of the day or night we knew that men could snatch us, hurt us and even kill us because of dad's old job. We kept a low profile for a very long time. I still attended school and kicked a football around but we had to stay quiet. To be seen was to be killed.

It was tough. Every child needs his father and I was no different. You need a dad to be around the house; to be there as a figure-head; to provide strength and discipline.

It meant that mum now had the jobs of two parents – and she was unbelievable. She did so well despite the turmoil going on around her. Mum's unconditional love and strength was incredible and we became so close.

But we never forgot that there could be a knock on the door at any time. That was always on my mind.

There were regular reminders of what could happen to us. On one occasion, they targeted a couple of dad's friends. They went straight through their front door, took everything they wanted and kicked them out. They didn't kill them but they ruined their lives. So we lived on the fringes and in the shadows. Nobody knew we existed. Not everybody survived.

I remember waking up one day and hearing crying in the lounge. Big crying. I walked in and mum and the rest of the family were weeping loudly. In Congo, when somebody dies you cry and mourn for a full day, then the body is brought into the house the next day and there is an open coffin for people to say goodbye before they are buried the day after.

I got up from bed and asked what happened. Somebody told me that my Uncle Llunga had been killed because the new regime found out about his links to dad. He had been taken outside and shot. President Mobutu had angered a lot of people and they were coming to gain their revenge.

That summed up how close we were to becoming victims of the uprising. We were living on the edge.

They accused my uncle of hiding dad ahead of his exit from Congo and that alone was enough to murder him. It is difficult to talk about. Me and dad have never really discussed it. It is too painful for the pair of us.

When I heard my uncle had been murdered it was just too stunning to believe. The shock was incredible. Mum was very emotional but once again she had to keep it together. I heard her crying all the time. She would weep in her room when she thought I couldn't hear her or in the day when she thought she was on her own. It was a bad time.

When dad left, the main guy in my life was gone. Life started to change. Fewer people came to the house and we realised who our real friends were.

People stopped wanting to be associated with the Muambas. I understood why because I knew they could get wrapped up in whatever the new regime had in store for us. But it just made us feel more terrified and alone.

The only positive from this kind of life was the way it shaped me. When you start to stress about the minor things in life you forget what matters.

Anxiety and worry are things you don't need. Try living with the threat of death hanging over you. Try getting to sleep at night when all you can hear is gunfire getting closer and closer to your own front door. You'll soon realise what matters.

#####

"Get up daddy, come on, get up," Joshua shouts, his tiny body reaching up for the TV screen mounted on the wall at home, as if he knows that I need all the help I can get. "Mummy, daddy is frozen, daddy is frozen – get up daddy."

Shauna is hysterical and panicking big time. Her mum, Marva, is over at our house and kicks in to protective mode.

"Maybe he just fainted," she says.

"Mum, this is serious – I can tell this is proper serious," Shauna replies. Her instincts are in overdrive.

She knows I'm dying.

#####

Without knowing it at the time, dad's departure had started the ball rolling on my new life in the UK. England gave both of us a new lease of life and a new opportunity. My eventual departure from Congo in 1999 was just as quick as my dad's had been all those years before.

Mum very quietly mentioned that I needed to go and get a photograph taken for a passport. I remember thinking that was strange. Why did I need a passport? I wasn't going anywhere. How wrong can you be?

We went into the centre of Kinshasa and I still didn't have a clue what was going on. Mum was laughing and joking at the same time and wouldn't tell me. We then went to the UK Embassy. Everything was pretty cool and relaxed. In a way, it was the calm before the storm.

A couple of helpers in the embassy addressed me in French as I couldn't speak any English at all and before I knew it the words they were speaking would be some of the most important I would ever hear.

"Hi Fabrice," they said.

"So you're the boy going to the UK?"

"What?"

That was the first I'd heard. I was badly confused by what I was hearing.

"What are you talking about?" I said.

The next thing I know I have a visa stamped into my passport and I'm heading to Europe.

Dad had been in a legal battle to allow him to stay in the UK and after being successful the first thing he did was apply for me to join him.

I had to sit down for a second and try and absorb all this. By the time it started sinking in I thought it was pretty cool. Europe sounded fun. Most of all it sounded safe. It was a chance for me and mum to get out alive.

But the next words spoken really rocked me.

"It's just you," they said.

No visa for mum. I was going on my own. That felt weird and sad but I must admit that I was too excited to let everything really sink in. I was young and selfish and I couldn't stop thinking about this big, bold adventure I was going on.

After receiving permission to join dad we couldn't tell anyone I was going in case somebody tried to stop me. It was still a dangerous time.

We got the visa on a Friday and on the Saturday mum took me for a haircut and bought me new shoes, shirt, trousers and a jacket. She wanted her baby boy to land in Europe looking his best. It was all a blur.

Everybody in Congo wants to come to Europe. They're obsessed with it – it is one step closer to heaven in some people's eyes – so mum was happy I was going but also obviously upset at the same time. Although we were sworn to secrecy, my Aunt Fifi was someone who obviously knew what was going on. On the Sunday, she told me to behave myself and be good.

During the rest of the day, I saw other family and friends who had no idea where I was going or why I was dressed so smartly. I was usually covered in sand and cuts from football and here I was dressed in all these new clothes with a fresh haircut. It was hard to keep it inside. Hard not to tell everyone, hard not to hug my aunties and uncles, to not let people know that I was leaving the country. It's the biggest secret I've kept in my life.

I will never forget my departure. I couldn't wait to see dad. I was excited as this was my first time on a plane. Mum bought me a ticket with money dad had sent back from the UK. From Kinshasa to Nairobi then Nairobi to London Heathrow, Kenya Airways.

As we left my house for the last time I had one last look around. I knew that would be it for a long time – and it was.

Mum put me in the back of the car and as we set off for the airport all my mates were walking towards our house to see if I was in, to see if I was coming out for a game of football. That upset me. 'I'm never going to see them again,' I thought to myself.

I slid down my seat in the car and thought about what was happening to me. I was so excited about Europe but that moment and those memories will never leave me. I was heading for a new life but I'd also enjoyed my old one too.

We left the house and mum was holding it together well. We got to the airport for the Sunday afternoon flight and she was ok. She was her normal self. The journey was uneventful, as if neither of us could quite believe it.

But that changed when I started walking to the plane. At the airport in Kinshasa you can see someone boarding their flight directly from the terminal. Mum was looking through the glass viewing gallery, blowing me kisses with tears running down her cheeks. I was the same.

I was only 11 years old.

First I'd lost my dad and now I was losing my mum.

One minute I was living in Kinshasa, getting on with life, moving forward and trying to literally survive. The next minute I'm landing at Heathrow. It is moments like these which made me as a man. Not many youngsters can have gone through that.

After my tears had dried, I remember sitting on the plane chilling and relaxing, checking out everything. I had a woman looking after me in Nairobi for a day, chaperoning me, before the flight to London.

Nothing thrilling happened on the flight, but as I got closer to London the excitement started to build. Now I was the most hyper kid on the planet. I couldn't wait to land, couldn't wait to see my dad and see what was happening.

The first shock hit me as soon as I stepped off the plane. Nobody had told me about the cold. My God, cold like no cold on Earth! Cold, cold, cold. As cold as can be. I can still shiver thinking about it.

When you get off a plane in a hot country you can feel the warmth seeping through the tunnel as you walk into the airport building. It was like that in reverse. This cold got into my bones big time. December in England – how could people live like this? It was a totally new and strange experience.

I put that to one side and sprinted through to get my bags. I just wanted to see my father after so long without him in my life. I was crazily excited.

I walked through into the arrivals and there he was. Tears flooded down my face. I'm an emotional guy and I sometimes find it hard to keep it together.

I'm back with my dad. I'm finally back with my dad.

He bent over and gave me a massive bear hug. He was clean shaven and he looked so smart and young. I remember thinking 'Does everyone in Europe look so good for their age?'

It was one of the most memorable moments of my life. That hug from my father will last forever in my heart.

#4

Culture Shock

IT'S hard to express just what a shock to my system London was. There I am, an 11-year-old African boy thrown into a new country. It might as well have been an entirely different planet. What was going on? We got on the Tube back from the airport and I couldn't believe there were so many people, so many sights and sounds, so many grown-ups crammed into one space.

This was not Kinshasa, that was for sure. My eyes must have been popping out of my head trying to take it all in. Two days ago my mum mentioned that I needed a passport photo and now I'm holding my dad's hand on the Tube in London, feeling the train rattling along, freezing cold, wondering if I was in some sort of exciting dream. It was unbelievable. We arrived at Lea Bridge Road in Leyton where dad lived in his two-bed flat. I looked up at my new home thinking how strange it was to be there. I was now a Londoner, for better or for worse. It was time to try and begin again.

After a month at home settling in, I was ready to face the big, bad world of school. Dad had enrolled me in Kelmscott School in Walthamstow.

I'll never forget it. If only somebody could've seen me that day. It was so different to everything I had known before. I was excited and nervous. I remember walking through the massive school gates thinking 'what is going on?' It didn't feel like five minutes since I was kicking a football around on a dirt patch in Africa and now there I was, in my blue jumper, white t-shirt and blue trousers desperately trying to dodge the puddles while people's mouths opened and closed with these strange noises coming out of them. In my head all I could think was 'why are you all speaking so fast?'

I walked into reception and the Head of Year 7 took me in and introduced me. It was the shock of a lifetime. The receptionist was talking to me but all I could do was just nod my head and grin. I didn't have a clue what she was saying. I stood there like an idiot. I was taken in to meet 7E, my form, and everyone was talking and shouting. It was just all so different.

Everyone's first day in a new school is a frightening prospect. Anyone who has done it will admit they would've preferred to stay in bed that day instead. Well, imagine trying to do it on a different continent with people talking in this crazy, weird language while the cold from the stone floors seeps through your school shoes. That's what I faced! The thought makes me grin wider than ever; it was all so insane.

I sat in the class, terrified, and all of a sudden this bell went.

What was that? What is the bell for? I soon realised it meant we had to leave our form room for class.

My new classmates were barging past and hustling their way through the corridors. I staggered around trying to understand the timetable someone had shoved in my hands. I eventually got some help from a boy called Cameron. I sat at the back of every class with a special assistant who could speak French.

She translated all the lessons in a tiny whisper, helping me to come to terms with the craziness around me. It wasn't easy. Back in Kinshasa I concentrated on just three subjects and used different coloured pens in my one notebook to work out which subject was which. In England, all of a sudden I've got what feels like 50 subjects to try and conquer, all with their own notebooks, textbooks and so on. I didn't think I could carry all of them never mind read them! Imagine going to university as well? Oh Lord...

However, as time went by, I slowly picked up the language and as I improved I realised one thing: my learning was way ahead thanks to what I had been taught in Africa. The stuff you learn when you are eight in Congo you learn at 11 in England, so I sped through most of the work. But there were still hiccups along the way. My teachers realised I was very good at maths but we couldn't talk about it because my English was so bad!

Bit by bit I got better. I slowly started putting sentences together so I could read small books but learning to speak sometimes worked against me. I remember once going on and on to dad about letting me go on a school trip to Barcelona. The chance to go there was too good to miss. Dad paid up and off we went.

When we got there I told everyone I could swim. "Watch me, watch me, I can swim, I can swim!" I just got carried away.

I couldn't swim then. I can barely swim now.

The rest of the class were shouting at me: "Fab, Fab, jump in, come on, jump in." I jumped in thinking I would be fine, only to realise that I was in the deep end. Half a minute of coughing and spluttering later and I was plucked out by a lifeguard who had dived in to rescue me. That was the end of my swimming career. At least it helped me fit in a bit more as everybody laughed their heads off. I just wish I could've found an easier way to do it!

That school trip also made me realise how much I truly loved playing football. I was obsessed with everything about it. There were a few year groups mingling on the trip so a ball would appear and we would all play together.

When you get away from school the classroom cliques disappear and we all joined in together. I loved the ethnic mix we had at our school. Some people criticise London schools for being too multicultural but ours was amazing.

All those different people from all over the world gave us an early understanding of the different kinds of cultures and worlds there are out there. We all learnt and respected our differences and religion and the different way of seeing things.

But football gave some of us the chance to come together. It was during those games that people realised that I wasn't a bad player. I faced older boys and did well. I realised you can gain self-respect and the respect of others from what you do on the pitch. It was a lesson that stuck with me.

#####

The stadium falls silent and still. The only movement seems to be the electronic pitch-side advertising hoardings which continue to rotate every few seconds sending out their message. Their bright colours seem at odds with the rapidly darkening mood. That stillness is broken as the pitch becomes littered with fluorescent saviours.

Dr Tobin mutters: "Oh my God, it's Fab" to himself as he sprints over to me. He is met at the scene by the Spurs doctor Shabaaz Mughal.

Dr Mughal has also seen me hit the deck. Again, he needs no second invitation. Again, he isn't officially summoned on to help. He is simply a doctor trying to save a man's life regardless of whether he was one of 'his' players or not. You're technically meant to wait for the referee to give you the nod before entering the field of play.

I guess the rulebook went out of the window 14 seconds ago.

#####

I didn't own a proper football kit until I started playing for my first Sunday team, Phoenix FC, in Year 8. My friend Cem had spotted me playing well on the yard and asked me to come along. I was bigger than everyone else and could head the ball so I did ok during lunchtime games. I could barely speak a word of English but he wanted me to try out. However, my first problem was that they played on a Sunday. There was no way dad would let me sacrifice church for football. But Cem's dad went round to our house and worked his magic. The next thing you know, as long as my homework was done and I still attended church, I could play. I couldn't believe it when dad said yes.

On the Friday before my debut I came home from school and on the kitchen table were a pair of football boots. Proper, actual, boots. Oh my God. I've never been so happy. They were a pair of Fila Eurocup II. I just couldn't believe it. I picked them up and sniffed them, turned them around and upside down, read the label inside – everything. They were black, blue and white with a big tongue that bent over. It was love at first sight. Every time I wore them I used to go straight home, wash them in soapy water, dry them and polish them before putting them under my bed. They were my pride and joy. I never, ever played in dirty boots – they were too precious for that.

That Sunday, Cem's dad came to pick me up and we travelled to some pitches in Leytonstone, right next to where the Olympic Park is now. I was proper nervous. I was about to play football in boots and on grass – actual proper grass – for the first time. I had my boots in my school bag and that was it. No shin-pads, no kit, no nothing. We arrived and I remember thinking 'this is it!' My English was still really bad so I couldn't really speak to anyone as I walked into a changing room full of lads I didn't know.

Anyone who's played any sport at any level knows that the first time you go to training or play a game for a new team is scary. I don't care what anyone says, you're always a bit nervous. Within a month you're all best mates but that first time never gets any easier. Well, on top of the usual nerves, try and imagine being a gangly African boy, easily the tallest in the team, thrown into a room full of kids speaking a different language to you. It wasn't easy. You could see everyone wondering who this new quiet kid was. Why was he here? Was he any good?

Then it got worse. "Here you go," the coach said and threw me my kit. You've never seen smaller shorts in your life. They were tiny! They didn't cover anything. But they were still part of my first football kit so I couldn't be upset for long. I felt like a million dollars in this red and black shirt, red shorts and red socks. Add in my blue and black boots and I had so many colours on!

They underestimated what I could do so I started on the bench and I was like every Sunday morning substitute in the country – freezing cold and bored. God, it was cold. I ran up and down just to stay warm, never mind trying to drop any hints to the manager. I pulled my shirt sleeves over my hands and shoved my hands in my armpits but nothing could put a smile on my face. The first half came and went, we conceded a goal and I was still doing nothing. I finally got on with 20 minutes to go. Little did I know, but something magic was about to happen.

I played at the back and was determined to show what I could do. I was fast and sharp and the first thing that happened was I nailed their striker with a great tackle – bang – before passing the ball off nice and calmly to start another attack.

You could hear the surprise on the sidelines. Maybe this big African boy could play. 'Maybe this big African boy should've started,' was what I was thinking. I got on the ball more and more until our left-back slipped it to one of our guys in midfield and I set off. As I went past him I screamed "give me the ball!"

Somehow those English words came out of my mouth. I didn't know where from. I must've picked them up at school and not even noticed.

"Give me the ball," I repeated. I was put through and I had a shot on goal from about 20 yards out. It flew past the keeper's right hand and went in.

Everybody jumped on me and we collapsed in a heap. There were only a few minutes left but I'd managed to score the equaliser and that changed everything in an instant. All these guys respected me now.

The next day when I walked through the school gates, people

wanted to know me. That African boy could play after all. All of a sudden I had loads of new friends, loads of guys keeping an eye out for me. It was the start of me opening up and becoming more confident. Everything started from there.

#####

"What is happening? Tell me he's not dead! Tell me he's not dead!" Shauna is screaming down the phone to Warwick.

"Let me ring you back in one minute," he replies, still trying to absorb what he has seen, still trying to pretend he isn't fearing the worst.

He has no clue what he wants to say, he just knows he needs to act, to do his best – the same as everyone else.

On the pitch I throw my new heroes a real problem.

I'm doing something called 'agonal breathing'. No, I'd never heard of it either. After a cardiac arrest you can carry on breathing for a short while without any heartbeat as your body continues to try and operate as normal before your oxygen meter hits zero. It's the caveman in all of us. Keep fighting, keep living, keep going until all the odds are so far stacked against you and the oxygen runs out. My body's reaction to what is happening is hardly helping though because it causes a tiny delay in my diagnosis, making it harder for those bent over me to work out what has happened.

But then, all of a sudden, it dawns on them.

Dr Tobin and Dr Mughal look up, my limp body underneath them, and exchange a look – a look that says: 'Is this happening? Are we going to have to start CPR in front of 36,000 people?

Are we going to have to use a defibrillator on a Premier League footballer?'

Yes guys, I'm afraid you are.

That look lasts a fraction of a second before they start the task of saving my life. They are slick.

Dr Mughal starts chest compressions, while Dr Tobin begins mouth-to-mouth – the first real person he has ever performed it on. What an honour. This is the guy I see on a day-to-day basis at our Euxton training ground.

We laugh, we joke, we mess around.

And now he's trying to save my life.

At the same time, Spurs' head physio, Geoff Scott, and Peter's X9 colleagues have poured onto the field while Mitch begins to sort the oxygen out.

Peter rummages through his oxygen bag and hands Dr Tobin a size four oropharyngeal airway, a small plastic tube which he shoves into my mouth to stop my tongue from blocking my airway.

The plastic is tough but necessary, its hardened edges scraping at my throat.

Dr Tobin doesn't ask for this piece of equipment and Peter doesn't offer it up. It simply appears, as if these two strangers have done this kind of thing together a million times before. There is some serious medical experience going on right here.

And this has all happened within 67 seconds of me collapsing.

These guys are slick.

#####

Halfway through Year 8, with my English skills getting better by the minute, I had another one of those life turning points when a kid called Rashid Kamara turned up at our school.

We clicked and connected from the moment we met. He was also from Africa – Sierra Leone – and he could play football. In fact, he was a serious player. He could also relate to me as an African in the UK and we became instant mates. We never left each other's side. If someone said "where are those two African boys?" everyone else would say "oh, you mean Fab and Rashid?" Sometimes in life you just meet a person you know you will get on with forever and that was what me and Rashid were like.

Unlike me, Rashid was very streetwise and he showed me the way things in London worked. He took me here and there, he protected me at times and we also grew as mates. There was nothing we wouldn't do for each other.

But if there was one area where Rash couldn't help out it was with mum. It's not as if I could just land at Heathrow and forget all about her. No son should treat his mother that way. But I was told by dad that she was in good hands so I tried to relax and just prayed that she was fine. Months flew by without me speaking to her. When we did finally speak, she mentioned that she had had to sell her house and move away. It was quite difficult for us both.

The situation at home had taken a turn for the worse after I left. Mum needed to keep a lower profile than ever so she moved even further out of Kinshasa. That was tough to handle. I was in London thousands of miles away and unable to help her in any way. I spent nights crying in my room, pretending to be doing my maths homework while lying on my bed, tears running down my cheeks. She was a very bubbly person but to hear her in that state of mind was really difficult.

After landing in London I didn't speak to her for so long but I suppose it was the way it had to be for all our sakes at the time. I was trying to adjust to a new life, which takes a lot of time and energy. Plus, we wanted to keep mum safe as well.

At the same time, dad was in a new relationship with my step-mum, Gertrude. When I first met her I couldn't really get my head around what was happening. She was already holding a baby, my brother Daniel, so I thought that was a bit weird but I just got on with it. I soon realised she was my dad's new wife. It was all a bit difficult.

I thought when I arrived in London that mum would follow us one day and we would all be a family again. So to see dad with someone else was yet another change I had to get used to.

Of course, I have absolutely nothing against Gertrude. There are no hard feelings at all because she welcomed me into her house. She was having to get used to me as well as the other way around. My mum is Christine and always will be. I love her like a son should love his mum but Gertrude has always been a wonderful step-mum to me and I have huge amounts of love and respect for her. She took me into her family like her own son and I will always be thankful and grateful for that.

But at the time it was just so different for me. I now had a new mum and a baby brother. Later on they would add Rachel and Ariel so I'm now an older brother to three people following an only childhood – I never saw that coming.

At least school was getting much easier by this time and my friendship with Rashid continued to grow by the day. We were just two young kids having a great time playing football, chasing girls, learning how the world works – the usual stuff really.

By the time we got to Year 9, Rashid was training at Arsenal because he was showing some tidy skills by then. Arsenal sounded like fun and I begged him for months and months to see if he could get me along with him. Just once. Just to see what it was all about. I pecked him so much until he finally told his coach, Steve Leonard, that he had a friend called Fabrice who could also play a bit.

Rashid managed to persuade Steve to come and watch us when we were playing for the school team. Arsenal had let some young players go so he had a chance to watch five minutes of one of our games and after taking a look he invited me down to Arsenal's Hale End training base, about five minutes from my house.

We were late for training that first night and Steve was waiting at the gate to let us know. It wasn't the best of starts. He told us to go and wait in the changing room. It felt like my first day at school again.

I was just sat there in a smelly pair of red shorts and a blue t-shirt with white socks and my Fila boots. There's this tall boy with shorts that aren't long enough surrounded by Arsenal's young-sters, all in their official training kit, nice boots and looking to-gether and sharp.

They could tell straight away that I was different and a few started ribbing me a bit. I didn't mind that and my experience at school had taught me that I could take anything. I wasn't intimi-dated; I just wanted to be like them. They just made me more determined.

The first session was taken by Arsenal legend Steve Bould and I kept coming back every Tuesday and Thursday. There was no real plan at the time, I wasn't even an official trialist and it wasn't

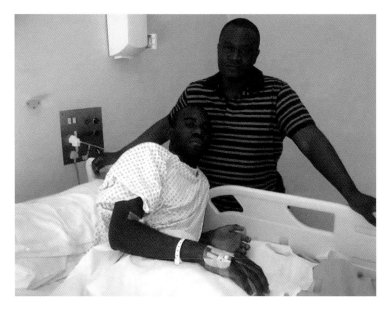

Father and son: Dad leaving so suddenly when I was young changed
my world, but I understand why he had to go

Happy together: Me relaxing with mum. My early childhood was full of laughter and love

Proud to be a Gunner: (Clockwise from top) relaxing in the club colours; in an aerial duel on my debut in the Carling Cup against Sunderland in October, 2005; appearing in Dennis Bergkamp's testimonial and in action against Reading in the Carling Cup at Highbury

City life: (Top) You can't beat the addictive thrill of first team football in the Premier League as I clash for the ball with Everton's Steven Pienaar

Ecstasy and agony: A goal against Blackburn Rovers in the final game (above) couldn't save us from relegation in 2008. Left: It finally sinks in that we are going down – a devastating feeling

Precious memories: Taking on Manchester United's Gary Neville and Anderson in 2008. I'll miss playing at awe-inspiring venues like Old Trafford, where it's so tough to get a result

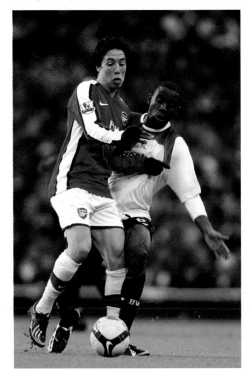

Happy returns: I always enjoyed going back to Arsenal, where it all started. Left: Closing down Samir Nasri during a Premier League clash in 2009. Above: Scoring against my old team in the Carling Cup in 2011

Team spirit: We looked out for each other at Bolton. Left: With Kevin Davies – a great leader – and my good friend Ivan Klasnic. Top: Gary Cahill – a future England captain? Congratulating him after scoring a goal at Goodison Park in January, 2012

Below: Keeping the inspirational Steven Gerrard quiet is no easy matter

Pride and joy: (Left) With newly-born son Joshua. Above right: Wearing England colours – I was so honoured to represent the country that gave me a new start in life

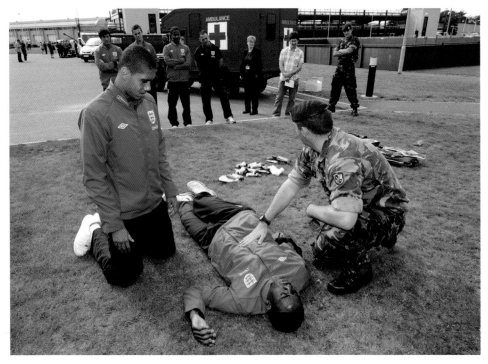

In the event of an emergency: Taking part in a first-aid demonstration with Chris Smalling during England Under-21s' visit to Colchester barracks in 2010. Little did I know...

Down... and out: March 17, 2012 at White Hart Lane...

Rescue mission: A shocked William Gallas bows his head as I receive treatment on the pitch

What has happened? The look on Owen Coyle's face says it all as the emergency services desperately try to save my life before carrying me off on a stretcher

as if a club like Arsenal just let anyone through the front door, so I was pleased that Rashid helped get me in. At the end of the season it looked as if I wouldn't be getting a chance to earn a proper trial and Steve broke the news to me. I'd been at the club for about six weeks but had never really proved myself or done anything to show them how much I wanted to become a footballer. I hadn't been lazy but I hadn't been brilliant either.

"Go away, enjoy your summer, come back at the start of next pre-season and I'll try and get you on at Leyton Orient or somewhere else," Steve said.

"But I want to play at Arsenal," I responded.

"Fab, I'm not sure that's going to happen."

I was upset and down during that time but I still needed to concentrate on my schoolwork and I just prayed with dad who told me to be thankful for having had the opportunity in the first place.

When we started back for pre-season I was the first one there. I was knocking on the door 90 minutes before anyone else arrived. If Steve wanted me there, and wanted to try and help me, then I felt I had to show how much I wanted it as well.

We trained on that first day and as the session came to an end Steve walked over and said "the boss is coming down tomorrow," meaning Liam Brady, the Arsenal head of youth development. "If ever you had a chance to impress him then this is it. Put yourself out tomorrow and show him what you've got – you never know."

An inter-club game had been organised so Liam could take a look at some other youngsters trying to make it. He had no idea who I was. By the end of the 90 minutes he knew exactly who I was. I took Steve's advice to heart and played better than ever.

I ran, chased, tackled and did everything to try and make Liam notice me. I played like my life depended on it.

When I was growing up in the Congo, it might surprise you to hear that I wasn't a rough tackler, in fact a lot of the time I was so scared on the pitch. I was just a nice kid who wanted to stay out of trouble. I used to get thrown off the ball really easily, pushed about and put in my place. When I was nine, I would be playing against 14-year-olds and African kids grow up very fast. Wow, it used to hurt.

That changed when I got to England. Something just clicked inside me. I wanted to win every 50/50, I wanted to prove my worth. Maybe I was trying to be the tough African kid or maybe I just wanted to be like the guys back in Congo who always used to show me who was going to run the show that day. It was never me that's for sure. So all this was inside me, helping me to prove a point in my trial.

After a while, Liam turned to Steve on the sidelines and it was clear I'd been spotted.

"I've been told Wimbledon have heard about him, they are interested and will try and sign him," Liam said. "He is a strong boy and he tries hard. Get him on an official six-week trial so we can have a proper look at him."

Steve came around and we had to sit in the front room for three hours waiting for dad to come home from work. I was so nervous because it all rested on what dad said.

He was worried about my schoolwork but I convinced him that I could fit everything in. Steve promised dad that my education would come first, just as it should, and that worked. Dad signed the trial form and I was in. That sealed my place at Arsenal for the short-term.

Now I was desperate to show that I should be kept on for longer. The door to a different universe had just been opened. It was all pretty cool.

#####

"Suzanne I need a bag packed – and quickly," Warwick tells his wife. He's heading to London. There will be no comedy club, no laughing tonight.

He rings Shauna back and tells her everything will be okay, to get on a train as soon as she can and that he will have a car waiting for her at Euston by the time she gets to London.

He doesn't tell her that he already thinks I'm dead.

You can't blame him for that – almost everyone else who is aware of what is happening thinks the same.

#5

Making It Count

AS I lie here, covered in hands and mouths and equipment, everything that needs to be happening is happening. You would think it would be organised chaos and that one man would assume control and try to get a grip on this madness. But, in fact, the opposite is going on.

The men trying to save my life are simply getting on with it; Dr Tobin is looking after his mini-department, Dr Mughal is doing the same, as are Mitch and Geoff.

All these men can think about is me. Their entire worlds have become this heap of bone and muscle lying in front of them. All of a sudden a pair of scissors cut and tear open my shirt before Peter sticks the automated external defibrillator (AED) pads onto my chest, making sure he doesn't touch the super-sticky adhesive along the way.

Let me repeat that. Automated external defibrillator pads are attached to my chest.

How did this happen? How come I'm dying on an early spring evening? What is going on?

The crunch moment arrives as the AED pads on the LifePak 1000 machine try and detect whether I can be brought back or not. I need something called a "shockable rhythm".

If I've got a shockable rhythm then that means there is still enough electrical activity in my heart to give me half a chance. Only the pads can analyse and detect it. Those battling to save me are helpless. As the dampness from the pitch begins to seep through the knees of their trousers, they await the good news.

Or the bad.

Whatever hope I've got will become crystal clear just moments from now. Above the silence of the crowd and the quiet efficiency of the men surrounding me, my fate becomes apparent.

"Place pads onto patient's bare chest," the defibrillator machine splutters out.

This is it. Long seconds pass by.

"Analysing now... stand clear... push shock button."

Finally some good news. The pads have found enough juice left in my heart to think it's worth giving me some serious voltage.

The shock button, the size of a 10p piece, glows orange as Geoff, the Spurs physio, prepares to get to work.

"Stand clear, oxygen away," he shouts, scanning up and down

my body to check nobody is still in contact with me before he hits the go button.

WHAM!

I receive a massive burst of electrical power – the first of 15 I will take before reaching hospital. I've now been collapsed on the floor for just two minutes and 21 seconds.

Despite taking the hit nothing happens.

Nick Osborne from the London Ambulance Service rushes onto the field, taps Peter on the shoulder and says: "We've made our ambulance ready for you mate, take it wherever you want to go."

X9 have their own ambulance at the ground but Nick has seen the need for speed and has already prepared a London Ambulance Service vehicle that can leave at any time.

"He's going to the Chest," Peter replies. 'If he goes anywhere but the Chest he won't walk out,' is what he is also thinking. Now is not the time to say that out loud though.

North Middlesex University Hospital is closer to White Hart Lane, less than two miles away actually, but Peter knows I need the specialist help the London Chest Hospital can provide. It has something called a 'cath lab' which is a mini-operating theatre full of all the equipment and knowledge needed to bring me back. What time I lose in going the extra distance will be made up by the extra expertise I receive once I'm there. Everyone is thinking ahead, thinking about what's needed to move me along the chain.

CPR is continued before the defibrillator is put to good use again, delivering shock number two.

WHAM!

This time there are signs I could be back. For a split-second I have three or four heartbeats before, once again, I slip under.

#####

During that six-week trial, my game improved. I was determined not to give Arsenal a reason to get rid of me. I was given my chance and I had to repay them.

As well as getting better I also began to feel more comfortable in my surroundings and I realised that my dedication was far better than anyone already in the academy. They had what I wanted to have and I was so hungry, so desperate to impress. I was like a maniac and worked until I could barely stand up. Steve made it clear that I had just six weeks to show I was good enough.

Eventually my hard work paid off and I was picked for a game against Spurs. The rivalry between the youth teams is the same as the senior sides – everyone wanted to beat them. I started the match and played well. I began in midfield and crunched a few of their players and showed my strength and ability. I ended up moving back into defence for the second half and enjoyed that too – I was playing well and showing that I could handle myself in more than one position.

Liam was there and you always knew that if Liam was at a game then there was something behind it and that you had better perform at your best.

I felt as good as those in the academy by now. I was no longer an outsider. They knew who I was and they knew I could play. My commitment was ridiculous – nothing was going to stop me now. Steve and Arsenal had given me this opportunity and I owed it to myself, but also to them, not to waste it.

At the end of the trial, Liam organised a meeting at Hale End and I had to take dad with me. I was so nervous about what was going to happen and the signs weren't good.

Before I went in, Rashid left Liam's office and he wasn't smiling. It was clear that he hadn't managed to get in. I thought that was the end for me right there. Rash was twice as good as I was but Liam had decided his chance was over. That made me even more nervous. We went into the office, near the canteen, and Liam was very straight and honest.

Fortunately – unbelievably – it was good news.

"We let your son go first of all but we've had another look and he's made a huge improvement," Liam said.

"We want him to join the academy. If he trains like he keeps on training then he will have a bright future."

I was buzzing so much. We all shook hands and I was just so excited. I tried to keep cool and act all casual but inside I was going mad. Dad was as relaxed as anything but when I got home I sang and danced and shouted in my bedroom. I was an Arsenal player! Ok, maybe not really, but that will change, just you wait.

After joining the academy, you have the chance to go in whenever you want and Steve offered to do extra work with me whenever I asked for it. I think he probably lived to regret that offer because I basically stalked him. As well as training on a Tuesday and Thursday I would also go in for extra training as often as possible, just turning up after school ready to work hard.

Not having Rashid with me was difficult because he was my friend but I had to try and forget that and concentrate on my future. Steve is a great man and anyone who has been through Arsenal will know him and will tell you the same. He knew how to work with me and how to get the best out of me. He understood me and helped to push me on. If I stumbled he picked me up, if I got mad he calmed me down.

I had more power and strength than anyone but technically I

wasn't as sharp as everybody else and both me and Steve knew it. If you want to be the best then you have to train harder than everyone else. It's really that easy.

And that hard.

In the academy the Under-15s trained on a Tuesday and the Under-16s on a Thursday and I got involved with both. Training with the older boys gave you a taste of what football was really like. On Tuesday Steve Bould would take the sessions and on Thursday it would be him and Neil Banfield.

If you showed hunger and improvement, you also got to turn out for the Under-17s who played on a Saturday. Their games were at London Colney Training Centre rather than at Hale End. If you played there, it meant you got to see the first team close up. That was a big motivation and it opened up the doors to some of the happiest times of my life.

#####

Those three or four heartbeats lift everyone's spirits. None of those surrounding my body are willing to give up quite yet, even though they are still fighting against the odds. They are too in the zone to hear the crowd chanting my name or feel the fear that is starting to whip round the stadium.

They don't see or hear Owen's first footsteps onto the pitch to see for himself that one of his players is in serious trouble.

They miss his brief chat with referee Howard Webb, who he first asks if he can come across to get a better look; they haven't got time to consider the crying in the stands, the hugging, the fear and the bewilderment, the open and unashamed praying on and off the field. They've got work to do.

#####

My first day at London Colney – oh my God! I remember getting a lift from Steve in an Arsenal minibus. He met me near the
bus stop near our house and had told me to be there at 8am. I
was ready and waiting by 7.15, decked out in my freshly ironed
Arsenal tracksuit with my boots. I was so excited I daren't miss
my ride. It seemed to take forever to get there. We had to go
past Tottenham Hale, Edmonton, Enfield and the M25 but it was
worth the wait. I can still remember when he pulled into the car
park – what a place!

It was a bright, blustery day and Steve told me I would remember it forever. He wasn't lying. The first team all had their
amazing cars on the right-hand side of the car park while we
had to go and park around the left-hand side where the reserves
were based. We went inside and it was a different experience – a
different world. We went upstairs into the first team lounge and I
couldn't believe where I was. I was in awe. I remember thinking
'This is what it is all about, this is so posh and it's only the training ground!'

I just looked around at how crazy it all was. The two sides of the
place were divided by a gym in the middle so the first team had
their area and the youth team had their own space too. But when
you went into the gym all the players mingled together or, if you
were me, stood around terrified. I was proper nervous. My heroes
were stood there in front of me. Thierry Henry, Sol Campbell,
Patrick Vieira – there they all were talking to the youth team and
reserve guys. Don't forget that those players were there every day
while I still spent a lot of time at Hale End with the Under-16s,
so I didn't have the confidence to say 'hi' to anyone. To me it was

unbelievable, I'll tell you that right now.

It was so different. At Hale End you had to bring your own kit but at London Colney it was already there ready for you. The first player I spoke to was Sol Campbell in the gym. He said 'hi' but I was so in awe of him I couldn't say anything. I just stood there.

He finally went "are you in the youth team?" and I said "yes" and that I was from East London. He was from Stratford so we got on and had something to try and talk about, even if I couldn't really find the words. He walked off and I just thought 'I know that guy from the TV'. It was all so strange and amazing. It still makes me grin today.

When the rest of the first team got there, the shyness really kicked in but then Ashley Cole arrived. He made me feel at home straight away. The more I started coming in the more they started saying 'hi' and nobody was better at it than Ashley. He had come through the system himself, he knew the pressures and the way you felt when you're surrounded by superstars and he did his best to make you feel comfortable; always laughing and joking with you and making you more confident. I have never forgotten his kindness towards me or the way he would try and include me in the chatter and the banter that surrounded the place.

I was still spending most of my time at Hale End but at least once a week I got to go up to London Colney. Bringing young guys into an environment that includes the first team is such an important tactic because it gives you a taste of what could be yours if you work hard enough. I wanted to be there. If you walk past the likes of Thierry and Ashley every day how can that not rub off on you, make you want to improve, to become a hero yourself?

Every time I entered London Colney it was just so completely different to anything else I knew. The car park had every type of car on it while I was still a schoolboy catching the 158 bus from outside my house before jumping on the train at Blackhorse Road Station to Finsbury Park, changing there for Cockfosters on the Piccadilly Line and then getting another bus to the training ground. Can you imagine what that was like? It was like going from rags to riches in 45 minutes flat. I used to go into school and tell everyone what was happening and they couldn't believe it. Neither could I.

At Cockfosters there is a tea shop and we all used to meet there. All of Arsenal's youth system has been through that tea shop. We used to throw toast and jam down and get ready for another tough training session.

Those older than me all had nice Armani jeans and Nike trainers and I thought how much I wanted to one day be like them. It gave me so much drive.

#####

My dad loves watching me play football and today is no different. He's at White Hart Lane with my brother Daniel and Alvin.

Dad never takes his eyes off me when I'm playing. Apart from today that is. As half-time approaches he can't hang on any longer and he dashes to the toilet.

Then all of a sudden he can hear the crowd chanting my name. 'That sounds like a lot of noise from Bolton's fans,' he thinks. 'Has Fabrice scored? I best get back to my seat.'

He went to the toilet 10 seconds before I collapsed. He has no idea what he is about to witness.

If you're going to die anywhere, die on a football pitch – that's my new motto.

Apart from a hospital it is the best place on the planet to be struck down because, as is happening right now, you're surrounded by experts straight away. I'll take all the luck I can get and another twist of fate plays out in my favour.

Andrew Deaner, a 48-year-old who first started watching Spurs 35 years ago, is sitting in the Upper East Stand with his brothers Jeremy and Jonathan. He is no ordinary supporter.

He also happens to be Dr Deaner, a consultant cardiologist at the London Chest Hospital. The very same place that Peter is planning on sending me to.

After cycling to the game from his home in Mill Hill, he expected a solid win for his side. The last thing he expected was to see his private and professional worlds collide.

"I should go down there," he tells Jeremy. "I could help."

Two young stewards block his first attempts to get down to pitch level. Who can blame them? They don't have a clue who he is. He could be some lunatic trying to snatch a moment of glory.

But Dr Deaner perseveres and finally gets lucky when he recognises a steward he knows. "Look," he says. "That is what I do for a living. I need to get on to that pitch."

The older, more experienced man ignores the guidelines and agrees. He tries to radio down for permission but cannot get through.

"Come with me," he tells the doctor. They race down the stairs and slip through a side door and before Dr Deaner knows it he's in a passageway near the pitch, coming out opposite the tunnel, heading towards me.

#####

Patrick Vieira is my all-time hero. I loved the way he played and the way he dominated on the field. But I didn't love the way we first met. I'd just finished playing in a game and had done ok. I was going for a dip in the pool when I saw Patrick coming towards me after he'd also been in the pool or jacuzzi following training. That is when the embarrassment started kicking in.

The thing is, I can kind of do a very good Vieira impression. I can speak like him, walk like him and I also look like him. I know that sounds weird but I just do!

So, there he is, strolling towards me by the side of the pool and I started panicking – this guy is a legend, my hero to end all heroes – and he shook my hand. All of a sudden someone has stolen my tongue, I couldn't speak. I coughed out a "hi" before he mentioned that he had heard about me recently. Me? Patrick Vieira had heard about me? What was going on? I didn't know what to say at all and just stood there as Thierry walked up behind Patrick and went: "Oh, so I see you two twins have finally met?" before walking off laughing. Oh my God, I was so embarrassed!

There I am, a schoolboy, shaking hands with a Premier League superstar and my favourite ever sportsman while stood half-naked by the edge of a swimming pool as the country's best striker dishes out the banter. It was all too much to take in. I went home and told dad I had met Vieira and that we had a conversation and the next day there he was playing on the telly. Again it was one of those moments when I thought 'hmmm, I need to get into this world on a full-time basis.'

I was surrounded by superstars and World Cup winners. It was just incredible and gave me the extra determination I needed.

Skill alone gets you nowhere. You needed the desire too and by now nobody on the planet had more than me.

The first time I met Arsene Wenger was when I trained with the first team. If you had played consistently well for the Under-17s then you got the chance to step up a level and enter big school. Not many lads get to do it but I had a run of good games and finally got the chance.

They only trained for about 90 minutes but it was so intense I felt like going to bed afterwards. Arsene had heard that I had been playing well so I couldn't wait and although I was allowed to get changed with the first team that day, I still went and got changed in the youth team dressing room. I was too scared to go in with all these Premier League legends.

They all started walking out to the field and I hung back, out of the way, not wanting to get involved too much. When you are young, it's easy to feel intimidated and nervous. Arsene got us into a huddle and gave us our instructions for the day. We worked on positional awareness and then had a game of five-a-side. I could barely keep up – it was so, so, so fast. The ball was pinging around all over the place. I was playing midfield but really I just wanted to play at the back so I could catch my breath and watch these guys.

Martin Keown played and he tried to look after me. He never shut up. I kept thinking 'Martin, stop shouting at me so much!' but he was a leader and everybody listened. Kolo Toure is a nice bloke and he also helped me out and Ashley was brilliant, as usual. He was always smiling and told me to keep focusing and keep enjoying it. You can't judge a book by its cover, you have to read it to make a judgement. Well, trust me, I know Ashley Cole and he is a good guy.

Thierry was unreal on the training ground as well. I noticed that he never tied his boot laces for some reason, while Dennis Bergkamp was just so cool and casual. If you ask any player from that time, he made the game look so simple; he made the hard things look so easy. He also did the easy things better than everyone else too!

What really surprised me was how competitive they were in training. Boy, these guys were tough on each other. Very, very tough. There was no messing about here, that was for sure. The players would be swearing and flying into tackles. It was a sign of their will to win. The intensity was so high. Pat Rice would run the sessions while Arsene stood back, watching. He let it be known what he wanted us to work on and would then just observe. His presence alone was enough.

For all this time I was continuing to keep dad happy by trying hard at school. I was so disciplined it was ridiculous. No homework was ever late, no teacher ever had a reason to discipline me and I made huge leaps forward. I was slowly becoming a player.

Suddenly, it was crunch time. Just before I was due to take my exams, Liam came to Hale End and told all of us in the academy to come in for a meeting and to bring a parent with us.

This was it.

We trained and then had a shower before waiting in the corridor, preparing to listen to our fate. Dad turned up in his shirt and tie and sat next to me while I prayed that I would be accepted as a YTS boy. I had worked so hard and had fallen in love with this kind of life. I wanted a scholarship so, so badly.

Liam finally ushered me in.

"We've been monitoring your son," he told dad, as my heart pounded. "He works very hard. He's the kind of person we want to stay around here with us. So we want to give him a YTS and pay him."

Wow.

I felt a burst of absolute joy, but the news didn't seem to affect dad. I was closing my eyes hoping and praying it would all come good and it had done. But dad stayed ice cool. He gave me his blessing but wanted to keep my feet on the ground.

All the hard work had paid off. I had been given a chance.

#6

Game Of Survival

FOLLOWING the nod from Arsenal, I had to try and calm down and get my qualifications. The YTS was one thing but that didn't give me the right to relax or not try my hardest in the classroom too. Arsenal made us work hard and revise for our GCSEs, which was the right thing to do.

When they got closer I went to my Uncle Paul's house, who is brilliant at maths, and he would work me into the ground every Sunday. I worked and worked and worked. In fact, I was so disciplined I found maths easy – I still love trigonometry and algebra. I passed my exams with no problems, getting an A* in French and all A-Cs, or so I remember. I never liked science but I managed to get through in one piece.

Before I knew my exam results I had the full summer ahead of me and I spent it getting myself into amazing condition. Boy, I trained like a lunatic. I was going to be a YTS player so I wanted to do myself justice.

On top of all the free gear we now received I also picked up £90 a week. Someone was paying me £90 a week – wow! I also got an annual pass for the London Underground, zones 1-6, paid for! I was always getting that out and showing off. This was all so new and amazing. I couldn't believe I was getting all this money for playing football.

The first time I got my £360 monthly pay I gave some to my step-mum to help her get something nice for herself. I felt untouchable. £90 a week plus a whopping £6 win bonus. I was a millionaire!

By the end of July I went in full-time to London Colney and my opening weeks were spent in a tired daze. We all used to meet on the Piccadilly Line train in the carriage behind the driver. If you want to see Arsenal's next generation of stars, go and stand in that carriage. It will be full of young lads asleep after being worn out by training.

When we started, Liam came in and straightened out anyone who thought they had already made it. He let it be known that the hard work started now. This was now my job. He addressed about 13 of us – from both YTS years – and left us under no illusions. Anyone not fulfilling their potential would not last five minutes. It was a good reminder of how far we had to go before we really belonged and could call ourselves footballers.

Being a YTS brought in loads of little differences. You were given two lockers to look after your personal belongings and in the dressing rooms EVERYTHING was laid out for us. Shirts, shorts, boots, towel – the works. I was so excited.

At the time, it was still pretty rare for youngsters to be given the chance to break into the first team. The only avenue appeared to be through the Carling Cup. In the year above me Johan Djourou had played in that competition and I was desperate for the same chance.

Me and Johan clicked straight away. Our lives were full of laughs and we were like brothers. We are still really tight to this day. It's the same with Quincy Owusu-Abeyie and Justin Hoyte. Justin became my taxi driver when I was a YTS boy because we both came from the same direction so he could pick me up for training. He'd be at my front door nice and early and we'd spend the journey being idiots, just like all boys are at that age. We all got so close and helped each other through. It was a great time in our lives. We went out at night in his car and would all go around thinking we were the coolest boys in London. I saw Quincy recently and he just laughed and said "look at you now" and we burst into tears of laughter.

As well as these guys there was another guy who was with us at the time. He was crazy. Bendtner. Nicklas Bendtner. He was the character to end all characters. He was so sure of himself and would say: "Fab, you don't need to tell me I'm good looking, I know I'm good looking" – crazy stuff like that. He was so entertaining and made the YTS experience so much fun.

Nicklas had a car and it started me thinking that I would like that. Now that I had a bit of money I started to think differently. But don't underestimate how hard I had worked to get there.

I didn't pay rent but I did give my step-mum money for Daniel and also my step-sister Rachel who had also been born by this time. I was their older brother, so I wanted them to be ok, even though I wasn't earning much.

#####

Dr Deaner has been on the White Hart Lane turf before, once during a charity bike ride five years ago with West Ham chef Keith Ross, a former patient, and once during a corporate day at the ground.

He could never have imagined that his hat-trick of appearances would be spent trying to bring a footballer back to life.

"I'm a cardiologist, can I help, have you got a line in?" he shouts as he approaches those working away on me. He feels stupid, stood there in his beige jacket and cycling trousers, but this is not the time to be self-conscious.

Both club doctors tell him that no drug line has yet been set up but that one will be put in place as soon as possible. At this moment in time nobody knows who this guy is, nobody can let him get hands-on just in case he's a nutcase. The last thing I need now is some crazy attention seeker making me more screwed than I am already. Who knew being dead could be so complicated?

For now, Dr Tobin is my lungs and Dr Mughal is my heart as I'm lost under a bunch of bright yellow jackets and team kit.

Peter, Dr Tobin, Dr Mughal, Geoff and Mitch have been joined by Nishal Juggessur, Richard Ferro, David Moran, Richard Mandy, Bill Halpenny, Terry Bourke and Paul Moran from X9 who have brought on all the equipment they can carry. It's like something off the telly as they begin to prepare the scoop stretcher in case I need to be quickly moved.

Peter, Mitch and Geoff keep supervising the AED machine, making sure the wiring and my oxygen tubes are all safely connected and working freely.

Dying because of a faulty piece of equipment is a big concern to these professionals – they all think I can be brought back, but only if they can keep the AED working properly.

'Don't die because of a malfunction,' Dr Tobin says to himself, his mind so focused on the job at hand that he isn't yet worried about my long-term prospects.

Other people are doing his worrying for him, including the players from both teams, as Webb begins to take control of the football side of things.

He consults his assistant referees Peter Kirkup and Michael Mullarkey as well as fourth official Chris Foy.

Along with Kirkup and Mullarkey, he has a quick chat with Spurs players Scott Parker, Ryan Nelsen and Rafael van der Vaart, as well as our captain Reo-Coker, and they all make it obvious that the players should leave the field as soon as possible.

They are not the only ones who need to move. I cannot stay here for the rest of the night. For the rest of my life. If I am to survive this then I need a hospital bed, not a football field.

Have you ever carried a big wardrobe or a couch or a bed? Of course you have. And I bet you didn't do it in silence either did you?

It was no different as those around me prepare to carry me off.

Dr Tobin shouts "ready, brace, roll" and I'm shifted to my left as the first part of the scoop stretcher is placed underneath me. He then repeats the shout as everyone involved rolls me to my right. My head twists and my cheek briefly touches the cold turf as the second part of the scoop is put in place and clicked together with the first.

I'm lifted and placed into a bigger and more secure stretcher. Just six minutes and 43 seconds after hitting the ground I'm on my way. But it's not easy. Three men on each side of the stretcher means 12 individual legs are at risk of getting tangled, 12 hands are grabbing at the edges, six minds all hope and pray that if I am dropped it isn't their fault.

"Steady... steady... slower... move to the left Pete... watch your back there... that's it... we're doing ok... ok, keep moving straight ahead," instructions and guidance fly in from all over the place as everyone concentrates on getting me safely off the pitch. Everyone is drenched in sweat while also juggling the oxygen kits and defibrillator equipment that are so important if I'm to survive.

As I'm moved towards the side of the pitch, Dr Mughal continues the constant chest compressions, refusing to stop, even for a second. There are many heroes out here and none bigger than him.

Imagine carrying that wardrobe, on a slippery surface, as someone stands virtually on top of it pressing down repeatedly. Then imagine doing it in front of half of London in person and most of the world on telly. Well, that is what is happening right now.

#####

Although this time in my life was great I continued to only have rare contact with mum. She wasn't mentioned much in the house by dad or Gertrude and I didn't want to bring her up in case it caused any frictions. Again, I lost touch with her for a while before I managed to get hold of her number.

I was so mad when I put the phone back down. Her conditions had got worse, she had moved even further from the nice side of Kinshasa to the real poor area. Tears flowed and I couldn't stop them. It was then that I made my mind up. I said out loud "I will do whatever it takes to see her, to make her life better." It was so difficult to hear how upset she was. In my head I thought people were hiding mum and her situation from me. She didn't know I was getting paid at Arsenal at all – that's how long it was since we had spoken.

I decided to start taking care of her. Behind dad's back I applied for a Western Union account and moved as much money to her as I could. Rashid showed me how to set up my account and took care of it all and I started sending her whatever I could afford. What can I say? I'm a mummy's boy. I wanted to make my mum happy.

God forgive me for saying this but in order to look after the woman who raised me, I also started selling my free Arsenal matchday tickets. I knew this was against the rules. I knew if I got busted I was on my way out of the YTS system super-fast. I knew a million people would feel let down.

But as far as I could see, mum needed the cash more than I did. Remember Arsenal v Manchester United, February 1, 2005? It was best remembered for the kick-off before the kick-off when Vieira and Roy Keane had a fight in the tunnel. I remember it for making the most money ever on a ticket. Someone paid me £500 – £500! – for a seat right behind the very same tunnel.

An hour and a half before the game I stood outside Arsenal tube stop, praying nobody would recognise me, shifting about in the shadows, when this guy offered me that much. The place was rammed with people on the way to the match – I couldn't fail to sell my ticket and I knew it. I also knew it was wrong but who could turn down that sort of cash? I had covered up anything I was wearing that could link me to the club but what if a youth team fan walked past? It was a gamble but I knew it was one I had to take.

In that split second I was on the verge of throwing my entire future down the drain. It would take someone 10 seconds to bust me if they knew who I was. I knew I was letting down everyone who had looked after me and shown such care and dedication in trying to help me make it but when it came down to what matters all that was forgotten, especially as I flicked through the fat wad of £20 notes in my hand, counting it over and over again, thinking about how much it could help mum. I only sold tickets when I really needed to and I didn't ever spend any of the money on me.

I'd seen worse things in my life than this. Mum was in a worse place than me so it was what I had to do.

And I would do it again now if I needed to.

Eventually I got hold of a picture of mum and I was really shocked. She had lost so much weight. It just wasn't right for her to be suffering like this, so I tried to help when I could.

At the end of my first year in the YTS I set myself the aim of making my debut and I knew the Carling Cup was the way.

By this time I'd started playing some reserve games for Neil Banfield. He was so hard on us but not in a bad way. We respected him. He was only tough on me because he wanted the best for us all. I'd watched guys making their debuts in the Carling Cup and that was now my goal. I was used to playing by now, I was up to speed and had the confidence and motivation to try and make it.

Also, I now saw the first team every day and that was important. I had lost my fear of the wider group. I was tall and gangly and stood out a bit so people noticed me and that helped me grow. When you do something every day rather than just a couple of times a week you can improve so quickly and football is no different. I grew stronger, my skills kept sharpening and I had more hunger than anyone I could see. This was what I was meant to be doing with my life. I was getting paid to hang around close to the Arsenal first team, watching guys like Robert Pires at the peak of their powers, trying to become them, to muscle my way into that universe.

You can't help but change as a person either. Quincy dressed like a model, he was draped in Dolce and Gabbana and Versace all the time and he looked really slick. Nicklas wasn't far behind. I hate to say it, but he can really put some clothes together. So different guys brought different styles and you wanted to try and keep up with that.

As well as being looked after by Liam and Neil, Steve Bould was also a massive influence as our coach. He was and is an Arsenal great and I learned so much from him. For a while, I was having trouble heading the ball so one cold day, on a deserted side pitch, he took me to one side and wouldn't let me leave until I'd nailed it. That man can head a ball! He showed me what he wanted me to do and when he headed this ball from near the edge of the box it kept on sailing until it landed just this side of the halfway line. Talk about leading by example. He helped sort me out and I was soon back to my best.

Then one day I was asked to train with the first team on a Sunday. Training on a Sunday seemed a bit strange and before I knew it I had been picked for our Carling Cup game against Sunderland at the Stadium of Light that week.

Pat Rice told me I was going to be involved after training. He took me to one side and announced the good news. I was so excited. I walked around trying to act cool, trying not to scream out loud. I just mumbled my thanks to Pat and got out of there as fast as possible so I could shout and dance. My step-mum and dad were very proud. We prayed together and I went straight upstairs into my room. I didn't do anything at all. I wouldn't leave the house or answer my phone. What if I got hit by a bus going for a walk? What if my mobile blew up in my hand? I couldn't risk it! I sat upstairs as the clock ticked down to the most exciting day of my life. Fabrice Muamba – First Team Footballer. Wow.

We took a private plane up north and I thought to myself that I needed to get hooked on this life. How had all this come by? How had it happened? It was all so much against the odds. I was on a private plane about to play for a Premier League club!

We got to the hotel and Arsene announced his team. I was starting. Amazing. I spoke to dad and he told me to do my best. We prayed together. I must have prayed about 10 times that day.

Sol Campbell and all the guys patted me on the back and told me I would be fine. Arsene just told me to keep passing the ball forward. He was concerned that I was passing the ball sideways far too much and he wanted me to keep the side moving towards their goal.

It was all so different. I walked into the dressing room with my kitbag tucked under my arm for the match and there it was – MUAMBA 44 – I can still see the shirt now. This is what I had worked so hard for. The nerves started to kick in as we started to warm up. And boy, let me tell you, did we need a warm-up. Sunderland is proper up north, it was October 2005 and it was freezing.

The noise when we walked out for the game was incredible. This was the big time, Arsene had already wished us good luck so there was nothing left but to go for it. Show everyone that I deserved to be here. A life already crammed full of adventure and a lot of tears was turning out great. I was so humbled to be playing and so grateful to get the chance.

When you watch the game on TV it's so different to being out there. For me I wanted to get a big tackle in so I would feel comfortable and I got Steven Caldwell early on and after that I felt like I could then start playing.

When they attacked the noise was crazy. Like being stood in the middle of a hurricane. I remember thinking: 'What is going on with all this noise?' We won 3-0 and it was simply a wonderful experience. I was hooked. After the game my Facebook page was going crazy and I had texts from everyone saying: 'Fab, you're in there now!' but I tried to remain calm. Let's play 25 games a season before we all get carried away. We flew back home and I got in late. I couldn't sleep until about 4am. My phone was melting with messages and all of a sudden girls are interested in me from all angles! I thought I was a player – in more ways than one!

Soon after the Sunderland win I played my first game at home when we beat Reading 3-0 in the Carling Cup and that was enough to convince Liam to offer me a professional contract rather than keep me on the YTS scheme.

I was agent-less and clueless so I knew I needed a bit of help and Warwick was the right man to show me what was what. He's done an amazing job for me. Arsenal offered me a two-year professional contract on top of the half a year I still had left to run on my original YTS deal.

I went from £90 a week to £700 a week plus a £20,000 signing-on bonus! £90 a week had made me do cartwheels so you can imagine what that kind of money did. Crazy, crazy, crazy. I kept sending some to mum, I gave dad some too and life was good. But then I did something really stupid.

Because I had played for the first team, I got a bit big time-ish. When we played Brentford in the FA Youth Cup, it went to penalties and I felt cocky enough to take one. I felt even cockier running up, so I tried to chip the ball down the middle. You've never seen a worse penalty. This ball sailed miles over the bar and we ended up losing. Oh my God. Oh. My. God.

The next day Liam called us all into his office and had a go at all of us. He saved an extra bit for me.

"What WERE you thinking?" he growled. "Please, just tell me Fabrice, tell me just what you were thinking?" The advice continued. "Next time don't bother being clever," Liam said. "Just pass the ball into the net." It was a good lesson learned.

If that wasn't enough, shortly afterwards Thierry gave me another reminder of who were the real men about the place. Arsenal were playing Portsmouth at home and Thierry got a penalty... and chipped it over the keeper. Everyone had heard about my nightmare, so he went running off around Highbury trying to find me in the stands, looking for the spot where the younger boys sat, pointing to his eye letting me know that the goal was for me! Liam looked at me and called me something unrepeatable. When I see him now we always laugh about it but at the time it was so embarrassing.

Liam was brilliant for us. He was the best mentor any of us had. We lost against Southampton in one game – and they were a decent side with Theo Walcott running the show – but Liam wouldn't have it. He tore into us again. He wanted us to learn responsibility and to take responsibility on the pitch. He pushed us hard, the only way it should be.

The professional contract changed a few things in the sense I now didn't have to start training until 9am rather than 8am. But the little perks didn't hide the fact that the intensity went up massively and even though I wasn't getting first team chances I felt I was in the right place to develop my game. Arsenal were a wonderful side and the facilities were out of this world. I was training with some of the best players on the planet.

I felt my time would come. I was still young and I was getting stronger. It was just a matter of staying confident and patient.

#7

On The Move

I'M carried past William Gallas who drops to one knee and prays. Bolton chairman Phil Gartside meets Webb at the edge of the pitch, as stunned as everyone else, searching for answers, searching for a way out of this mess.

Owen and Spurs boss Harry Redknapp have a touchline conference with Webb, Foy and players from both sides.

"We can't play this game now," Owen says to Harry. "My guys need to know how Fabrice is."

"Owen, Owen, I'll do whatever you need, whatever you need," Harry replies. From the moment I collapse Spurs are with me every inch of the way.

Harry will ring Owen every day until I'm discharged, checking on my condition, checking that Bolton don't need anything doing. He is one of many I will never be able to repay in full for his kindness. Owen didn't see me fall, he just looked back across and saw me on the ground. He doesn't know what is going on, all he does know is that the sound of both sets of supporters singing my name is making the hairs on his neck stand up.

FABRICE MUAMBA! FABRICE MUAMBA!
FABRICE MUAMBA! FABRICE MUAMBA!

He is a devout Roman Catholic and he begins to say his own prayers, prayers that are far more important than any team talk. "Let him live, let him be well," he says to himself. Pull through. The game looks like it will be cancelled. How could it not be?

A 23-year-old is dying live on television.

I finally leave the arena, an unrecognisable shape lost among bright yellow coats, overworked doctors, incredible paramedics, devastated footballers, shocked officials, heartbroken fans.

The last sound as I'm carried down the White Hart Lane tunnel is the applause from both sets of supporters. The noise is ringing in everyone's ears.

I wish I'd been around to hear it.

#####

At Arsenal, not everything was going according to plan. Nailing down a regular first team place was not easy. By the end of the 2005-06 season, any chances of breaking through seemed to be slim and Warwick advised me that it was time to start thinking about moving on loan. I was 18 by now and it was time to get out there. A loan spell meant I could still remain an Arsenal player while also getting some game time in.

Warwick spoke to Birmingham City who had been relegated from the Premier League and they seemed an ideal fit. It seemed a good challenge on a personal and professional level. I moved out to Birmingham and had to set up my new life. Dad and my step-mum were ok with me going but they wanted me to come back at weekends to see everyone. There was no doubt it would be tough early on. I was a London boy but I soon adapted.

I met Warwick at Birmingham New Street station and we went to St Andrew's to sign some paperwork with Karren Brady, who was very welcoming. She looked after me brilliantly when I was there, I have nothing but respect for her. It was all such a whirl-wind.

The next day we trained at the stadium and I met all the players, along with the manager Steve Bruce. I really enjoyed working with Steve. He just knew straight away how to work with me. On the training ground his face used to go so red – bright, bright red – when he was trying to get his point across but he always managed to do it.

Steve was a great man and a great character to play for. Friday was Steve's day, Steve's time to shine, to show us he was still a player. He used to milk it and never took it too seriously.

As we left on a Thursday he would announce which player he was going to be in the Young v Old game the next day. "Fab, son, I'm going to be Cantona," he'd say, running his fingers through his hair. "Either Cantona or George Best. I've not made my mind up yet." He'd be Cantona or Maradona or Pele or one of the greats. He used to put himself out there for us to laugh at and laugh with. That's what being a manager is about in my opinion – being relaxed and making it enjoyable for the guys.

Steve used to run about for about five minutes and that was it – then he'd just stand up front for the rest of the session, catching his breath. "This is what top strikers do," he'd shout. "I'm in the right position." Friday was only a light day so it was always fun. You could tell Steve had played a lot of football. He still had a good touch and you just knew he had been a player.

At one stage, Steve asked me if I knew anyone who he should go for at Arsenal who wasn't playing in the first team regularly. I jumped at the chance to mention Nicklas and Seb Larsson and they soon joined me in Birmingham.

Nicklas was an instant hit because he scored in his first game and Seb also did a good job. On the flip side to that, I spent the first month on the sidelines and I got so frustrated. I started to regret going there. I can throw a tantrum when I don't play and I threw a real one here. But Steve calmed me down and promised me that my time would come – and it did.

I eventually settled into the first team and I ended up loving the 2006-07 season. I just made tackle after tackle and the fans took to me, which was great. They even made up a song about me that still makes me laugh my head off: 'MUAMBA, WHOOOAH, MUAMBA, WHOOOAH, HE WAS A REFUGEE AND NOW HE'S QUALITY'. Ha ha, I loved that! Don't believe it when a player says he doesn't love hearing his name chanted, it is a great feeling.

We eventually managed to get back into the Premier League at the first opportunity, finishing second. We topped the table and had a chance to win the title but Sunderland pipped us to it. Steve used me wisely, picking me for a few games and then telling me to disappear for a day or two to recharge my batteries.

I started going out to nightclubs in Birmingham and because it was a small city, it soon got round that we were lads who enjoyed a good time. I started getting in trouble with girls who heard I was speaking to other girls on the same nights out and all that. They all seemed to know each other! It wasn't fair and also so confusing. I would take a girl to Nando's and then her friend would find out and then her friend would find out and so on. It was all too much! I was only drinking a small amount after a Saturday game. We would go to a soul bar and a place called Bambu. We couldn't be cooped up all weekend, we had to let some steam off some time. A night out is not a crime for the rest of the world and it shouldn't be for footballers – as long as you respect yourself, others and the boundaries of how to behave properly. Me, Neil Danns and Cameron Jerome all enjoyed going out and having a look around.

Towards the end of the season, Andy Cole joined us on loan from Portsmouth after Steve decided that we needed some experience during the run-in. I didn't believe it when I heard he was joining. I walked straight over and shook his hand. "I'm Fabrice, nice to meet you," I said before starting to really bug him. Man, I bugged him so much! "How was life at United? What was it like to play at Old Trafford all the time?" I couldn't shut up but he showed me respect and answered me patiently. He is a down-to-earth man, an unbelievable footballer and somebody I have a crazy amount of respect for.

During that year at Birmingham I even started an Open University course in maths and statistics. You always need a Plan B in life. Nobody at the club would believe me. "You? Whatever, shut up," was usually the response I got. A lot of the guys saw the smile and my laidback nature and forgot who was underneath. I thought I needed to back myself up in case I needed it, even if I was too busy in the end to finish it.

We got promoted at Preston North End that season. It was a great feeling. I didn't play at Deepdale that day but I went on the pitch at the end and the crowd chanted my name. It was fantastic. So emotional.

#####

"Let's go inside, let's have a chat inside," Howard says to both managers. He knows the game cannot continue but he needs a quick and quiet conversation to confirm that.

As we head down the tunnel my stretcher is placed on a trolley as the efforts to revive me continue. The trolley hadn't been brought onto the pitch as there were concerns it would get stuck in the mud.

Each side's club doctor is still running the show and a third shock is administered. Still nothing. I'm being as stubborn as ever.

In the tunnel the gaffer and Mr Gartside are just two of many bystanders, all trying to get their heads around the fact a young man, at the peak of his life, is dying in front of them.

Stewards surround the situation, ensuring the guys working on me have the space they need.

Owen, Harry and Howard head towards the officials' room and they have a chat in the corridor, Owen straining his neck back towards the tunnel to see if he can still see me as I'm pushed towards the ambulance.

"Whatever Bolton want to do is absolutely fine by us," Harry says as he repeats his earlier support. "We understand the situation Owen, we'll call it off," Howard replies.

Owen thanks the pair of them but his mind is elsewhere. He has to dash back to the dressing room to try and get an update, to see how his players are. To see how his player is.

Dr Tobin is still giving me oxygen and Dr Mughal pounds away at my chest as Peter heads off to the ambulance, making sure its tail-lift is down and its back doors open.

WHAM!

Shock number four is received on the tail-lift of the ambulance. Most people are dead and gone by now. I might be dead but I'm not quite gone, thanks to those around me.

#####

The support from Birmingham's fans backed up the decision to leave Arsenal, even though I hoped to return there to continue my career.

I called that one badly wrong.

I went back to London during the summer and went in to see Arsene. He was fantastic with me and very honest. He took me in his office, looked me straight in the eye and told me the truth. "I can't promise you first team football," he said. "You're at the stage where you've been playing regularly and you've been playing ever so well. I can't guarantee you any chances here because I've got too many players." Fair enough, he was right. He did have a lot of players. "Good luck," he said.

We shook hands and I left. It was as straightforward as that. Once the decision was made I was fine with it. I didn't want to be back in the reserves. First team football gives you a buzz and when it's taken away nothing matches it. Birmingham had been promoted and I was a fans' favourite there, so it seemed the right decision to make a full-time move to the Midlands.

I'm not going to pretend it wasn't difficult at times because I had supported Arsenal as a boy but that is the way things sometimes turn out. It was hardly life and death. And I think I'm fit to judge matters on that score. It was a case of steering my life in a slightly different direction while always moving forward.

I couldn't wait to get started and play in the Premier League. I wanted to play. I wasn't one of those who wanted to collect money for nothing. Forget that.

When Birmingham got promoted, the attention started getting serious. All of a sudden we'd go out and there would be media interest and people chatting to you in bars. You have to keep cool and surround yourself with good people. If idiots are telling you that you're the best thing ever then eventually it's going to sink in and change you. I made sure I stayed focused, humble and low-key. You never saw me at a perfume opening or a restaurant night. Dad kept me grounded and Rashid also told me the truth about life if I ever needed telling. If you want to be fed bullshit you can be fed it all day. If you want to stay true to yourself then you need to surround yourself with people who will make that the case. Honesty is the most important thing. You need to be kept straight. That leads to a decent, simple life which is uncomplicated. Bullshit leads you into temptation and trouble.

I moved to Birmingham in a great deal for me that saw my pay rocket to £10,000 a week. For real? Are you actually kidding me? For playing football? Someone pinch me. I also picked up a £2,500 appearance fee and a healthy signing-on deal plus a win bonus.

Warwick had spoken to Karren, sorted it all out, then rang me and said: "I've got the best option for you, trust me – this is a great move." He then mentioned the money and I think I must've almost fainted. A boy from the Congo earning that much? Wow. I went straight to the cash point, stuck my card in and checked my balance. Is this all for real? Yes it was.

That sort of money bought me my dream car – a Range Rover – but I also did a more important thing, which was send even more cash back home. My Aunt Fifi, mum's sister, moved from South Africa to Manchester around this time and that gave me a more direct link to mum. It meant contact with her was easier to sort out. I was sending £3,000 a month to make sure she had all she needed. Plus, some Premier League games are shown in the Congo so she was able to see me play, which I hadn't expected. To speak to her over the phone was great but I started really wanting to see her, to show her that I'd made it. I hadn't seen her for years by this time. I never told dad about seeing mum, I didn't want anyone else involved in that – it was my problem to sort out.

By this point, the girls were really starting to throw themselves at me. It was ridiculous. If you don't keep your head in that situation, then you can get in trouble quickly but I managed to be ok and steered a pretty smooth path through all of that. Well, almost smooth. I coped by pretending my name was 'Marcus' when we went out. That meant nobody hassled me. I had more important things to concentrate on. And that thing was the Premier League.

We lost on the opening day of the 2007-08 season 3-2 to Chelsea. It was just so humbling to be on the same pitch as Michael Essien, Frank Lampard, Didier Drogba and the rest. I must admit I was scared early on in the game – I was daunted by the occasion. I couldn't even do my usual trick of banging someone early on because I couldn't get near them! The speed and the skill involved in the game was like nothing else I had ever experienced. It was a different world and technically a real step up. You have to be sharper mentally and physically.

Then, with only a few months of the season gone, we lost our manager. I was shocked when Steve went. I don't know all the details about what happened and I texted him to say that he was one of the main reasons I had signed. He was loved in the dressing room and we wanted him to try and help keep us up. He went to Wigan Athletic and was replaced by Alex McLeish, who had just quit as Scotland boss. He was a good tactician and manager but we just couldn't seem to get any consistency. Win, draw, win, lose, lose, draw, win, draw and so on. We couldn't string together enough positive results to ever really get the season going.

I remember we played Derby County at home in February and were winning with a minute to go and Emanuel Villa scored an equaliser. I remember walking off thinking 'how did we just let them score?' We just couldn't get going or keep a clean sheet.

As the end of the season got closer and we looked really screwed, we had to go to Villa. We only had four games to go and the pressure was incredible. Birmingham is a pretty small city and everywhere you went in the build-up to the game there would be people letting you have it. I was in a lift in the Bullring shopping centre one day when a fan laid it on the line. "You've got to get a point this weekend," this bloke said. "If you do nothing else, don't lose." Everyone from your neighbours to the guy at the petrol station would get on to you to win. I knew the Birmingham/Villa rivalry was big but I didn't know quite how serious it all was until we were in the deep end.

The game came around and it was horrible. We got smashed 5-1 and couldn't get near them. Not only were we humiliated in the local derby but it also took us a step closer to the drop. Horrible. They were better than us in every department and I was as much to blame as anyone. I came up against Gareth Barry that day and he was sharper and better than me. He controlled the midfield and made me chase him. He was very smart. You have days like this in football. I was still very young at this time. He made it look easy while I did the opposite.

We were 2-0 down at half-time and Alex raised his voice in the dressing room. He demanded that we show more desire and determination. But you can only do as much as you can at times. Villa were just too experienced and too good that day. We went back out for the second half determined to perform and then John Carew scored quite soon after. Bang. Game over. A goal after half-time is an absolute killer. You come out pumped up with the manager's words in your ears and then it's like a balloon bursting – you just lose all that motivation in a second.

After the game I got out of there as quick as I could. I just wanted to hide. Forget the relegation threat, it was the local embarrassment that got to me more. I locked myself in my place trying not to remember the words of one fan I saw on the way out of the stadium. "Muamba, tell them none of you were fit to wear that shirt," he said. "None of you." I have no problem taking stick off fans because football is not cheap and fans pay their money and have a right to their opinion.

I knew at that point that we were in deep trouble. Serious stuff. We played Liverpool next and we should have won. 2-0 up became 2-2. Deeper trouble.

We then had a massive match against Fulham. They had pulled off an amazing win against Manchester City in their last game which meant they were still – just – in the Premier League, so they were buzzing. It was goalless at half-time and Alex made it clear that a point would be a great result. Get a point here, win our last game and see what happens. He was right, all we needed to do was have a strong defensive performance second half and we leave with a point. Seven minutes after the break Brian McBride scored. That kicked the life out of us and we ended up losing 2-0.

It meant that, aged just 20, I would be playing in a classic relegation battle. We had to beat Blackburn Rovers on the final day and hope that Reading and Fulham slipped up. We held our part of the bargain. They didn't.

We were brilliant that day. A 4-1 win and St Andrew's was ROCKING. I've never heard a noise like it as we walked out for the game. It made you tingle. David Murphy gave us the lead and I thought the stadium would fall down. We had a slight chance of staying up but news soon got around the stadium that Reading were winning against Derby and although we won comfortably in the end thanks to two from Cameron Jerome and an injury-time fourth from me, we also knew that Fulham had beaten Portsmouth. We were down.

When you get relegated it's a funny feeling. You're obviously gutted but your main thought is 'where could we have got another point, another win, another draw?'

It's not so much anger as trying to think back to the tiny details that could have added up. That shot you missed, that stupid booking that stopped you from flying in for the rest of the game, that bad clearance that led to a goal. When you're relegated by just a point it's the cruellest feeling in the world. You just want to get away. You've failed at your job. I would've done anything to change what had happened.

We were finally down and I knew quite quickly that it was time to move on as a player. I loved my time at Birmingham but what fans need to understand is that when you've sampled the best league in the world you want more of it. The Premier League is addictive. Players leaving a relegated club aren't leaving it for the cash, they're leaving it for the fix they get playing against the best. It is that 90-minute high they chase, not the extra money. I was no different.

If you go to St Andrew's now you will still hear my song. I gave my all for the club and it's nice to be remembered as someone who played hard. Birmingham gave me the opportunity to express myself and to become a proper footballer. I had dedication when I joined the club but no experience. My time there changed all that. I will always be thankful to the club and the way they took a gamble on a young kid who didn't really know much. Karren and Steve and Alex and everyone there will always be respected by me because of that time. All footballers can point to a period in their life when they can say they grew up on the pitch and my time at St Andrew's is when it happened to me.

#####

Dr Tobin, Dr Deaner, Peter, Paul Moran and Anthony Dorrington all clamber on board the ambulance with me but for now it's heading nowhere. Anthony is one of the crew and he knows you can't just throw someone on the back and head off straight away.

These guys have got work to do, securing my situation, hooking me up to a machine that can monitor oxygen and carbon dioxide levels as well as securing all the drips and equipment safely.

Trying to do important medical stuff on a rocking ambulance

is not easy. It makes far more sense to sort me out in the car park and then get moving once I'm stabilised. Or hopefully stabilised.

The ambulance doors clang shut and all of a sudden the noise and the panic of the outside world is replaced by the calm efficiency of these experts doing what they are paid for.

The hassle is gone, the people peering over the doctors' shoulders have disappeared. The real work begins now.

My feet dangle close to the end of the stretcher, my brow still contains the traces of sweat that come with 41 minutes of playing midfield against one of England's best teams.

All of a sudden more plastic is shoved down my throat as Peter fits a size 5 laryngeal mask down my airway to get a better supply of oxygen.

The earlier bag and a mask that's been over my mouth are not the worst things in the world but Peter's handiwork means the oxygen I'm now receiving is far, far better.

As he sorts me out the ambulance side door opens up. Dr Mughal is stood there with Dr John Hogan, another cardiologist who was at the ground.

Another cardiologist who also happens to work with Dr Deaner every Monday at the London Chest Hospital.

Small world.

The two friends share a smile, wondering at the way fate has led to this position.

"If you work at the Chest," Peter says to Dr Hogan. "Ring 'em, we're coming in."

"Yes, no problem," Dr Hogan says as the ambulance door is closed again.

He gets on the phone and the London Chest Hospital prepare the red carpet.

There's no room on the ambulance for Dr Mughal – he has already done more than I will ever be able to thank him for. My life now rests on those inside this confined space. I hope it's not my coffin.

#8

The Call

AS well as trying to sort a career as a domestic player, trying to fight back against the huge odds against me, I also had one eye on representing England. From an early age I'd been involved at some stage, all the way from the Under-16s through to the Under-21s, who I represented at both the 2009 and 2011 UEFA European Under-21 Championships.

Playing for England has given me some amazing memories and some great friends. Mark Davies, James Vaughan, Lee Cattermole, Mark Noble – all these guys have done well in their careers and it's been easy to see why having spent a lot of time with them on international duty.

As far as I'm concerned playing any international football is a massive honour and it is an interesting chance to get away and see other things, other players and other set-ups. I made my Under-16 debut against Wales at Barry Town's home ground in November 2002 and I remember thinking to myself 'I want more of this.'

Not just the opportunity to play but to also get out there and see for myself what competitive football is about.

I was only a 14-year-old at the time, nothing more than a kid, but playing in the England set-up so early on gave me the confidence and belief that I could make it; that I could take those new experiences and learning opportunities and bring them into my game.

It was around the time I started representing England that I started to grow such strong feelings for the country. The two are definitely linked. My language skills were improving constantly and I was getting the chance to travel around the UK, seeing different parts of it, speaking to new people and expressing myself in different ways. It was the making of me.

All the way through my career I was always determined to be available for England because I knew it was helping to develop me as a player and as a person. Here was a country that owed me nothing but had given me everything. It had saved my father's life and given him security, a home and a job, it had educated me and it had helped save me from the fear and uncertainty of growing up in an African country that was becoming increasingly desperate.

You go to America and see for yourself. Or France. Or anywhere else. No other country in the world gives you the same opportunities to make yourself a better person. Everything I could ever wish for and want has been provided for me by moving to England. You have to be appreciative in life and to stop and think and give praise when it is due. Nowhere deserves more praise than England so the least I could say is thank you and to try my best on the pitch.

I was determined to give something back, to show that whatever life I would've led in Congo was nothing compared to the one on offer, as long as I worked hard, prayed and did me and my family justice. I wanted to pull on an England shirt to show my gratitude towards my new country.

By the summer of 2007 I had become a real contender for the Under-21 side, the one team you really want to play for at youth level. I like to think my performances for Birmingham that year not only helped get us promoted but also guaranteed my involvement in the national team.

As the 2007-08 season arrived on the horizon and as Birmingham prepared for their trip to Chelsea, Steve Bruce got us into a huddle at training. It was a Friday morning and he said "good luck to you guys off on an international week and, by the way, somebody's off to the Under-21s."

He looked slowly around the group and all our eyes followed him. I was trying to guess who he could be about to give the nod to. I couldn't wait to congratulate the lucky guy who was going to play for his country.

"It's you, Fabrice," Steve then said.

I just went "really?" and the whole huddle burst into laughter and started shaking my hand because of how shocked I was. I was totally buzzing and I couldn't wait to tell dad. Here's me about to play for the England Under-21s against Romania. It was another unbelievable achievement.

"You're a footballer now," Olivier Kapo said, delivering his line with a big grin. "Congratulations. You can say you're a footballer.

Make the most of your chance." I already thought I'd produced a lot in my short career and considered myself to be a footballer already. Little did I know that Olivier had a point – a point I would finally understand shortly afterwards.

I was so excited by the whole experience. I grinned wildly when I received an email to officially confirm my place as well as a letter to congratulate me on being selected. It was Stuart Pearce's first full-time game in charge.

Peter and Dr Tobin carry on their basic life support as Dr Deaner starts to insert a catheter into my groin, accessing my femoral vein, one of the best parts of the body to inject drugs nice and quickly.

He hovers over me and wipes my skin with an alcohol swab to try and remove its clammy, sweaty feel. I'd apologise if I could. He is then distracted briefly as he suddenly remembers he's got no medical gloves on.

He quickly searches the ambulance until he finds a pair and hits his spot, sinking a brown Venflon line into me which will allow him to start giving me some serious juice.

I'm immediately given adrenaline in the hope that it will be enough to get my heart working again.

Not today it's not.

Dr Deaner is then passed 300mg of Amiodarone by Paul, a wonder drug for those who have failed to respond to CPR and defibrillator shocks.

It sets to work trying to stabilise the cells of my heart, trying to fix abnormal rhythms, trying to get me out of this mess. My electrical activity is all over the place and it needs to calm down. Amiodarone is the drug that is meant to make that happen.

It does not make that happen. I'm still gone.

The last time I checked, I was playing in an FA Cup tie and now a complete stranger is injecting drugs into my groin. How did this happen again?

Twenty-one minutes after I go down and we're ready to leave White Hart Lane. Usually someone is just about getting their initial treatment by now and that's if they're super-lucky. Don't even ask me how fortunate I am – the numbers are off the chart.

Peter places a 'blue call' into the London Ambulance control room to tell them that we're about to head off. He's talking about someone who sounds familiar.

"23-year-old male in witnessed cardiac arrest," he shouts down his radio. "He's had four shocks but is still in VF, he's intubated and undergoing full drugs protocol."

He turns to Barbara Mackinnon, the ambulance driver, and gives her the thumbs up. "Nice and steady," he says. "Let's take it nice and steady."

#####

The England game was at Bristol City's Ashton Gate ground and they sent a car to Birmingham to pick me up. A nice BMW 7 Series arrived at my house and I remember thinking how great it all was. The call-up, the official letter, the car to take me there. It was all so far removed from my early life.

We had such a good team then and England's Under-21 strength was pretty clear when I turned up at the hotel. Stuart Pearce was there in reception and welcomed me to the squad. I went up to my room in my Birmingham tracksuit before then coming down to lunch where everybody was present.

The scale of England's talent was there for all to see. The likes of Joe Hart, Gabriel Agbonlahor, Mark Noble, Theo Walcott, Tom Huddlestone and James Milner were all in the dining room. That made you realise how serious this all was. All the other guys got on well and a lot seemed to know each other from earlier meet-ups or from playing against each other a lot. Everyone made me feel so welcome. We all got on well. We just chilled that first night and watched TV, nothing too exciting before starting training the next day.

The whole environment was very welcoming from Stuart at the top, all the players and even the kitman, Pat Frost, who made me feel as if I belonged straight away. Anyone who says they don't or can't enjoy international football because of the pressure of trying to fit in and gel with the squad is talking rubbish. I got nothing but respect and a friendly welcome from everyone.

When it came to the match I was nervous but also massively proud and excited. I started on the bench and watched Matt Derbyshire give us an early lead before Stuart decided to introduce me shortly after the start of the second half.

I tried to go through my usual rituals – warm up properly, get my studs checked and so on – but all I could think about was my excitement and my desire to get out there and play football. It can be as simple as that at times. Just get out there and strive for the win.

I replaced Michael Johnson with Stuart's instructions ringing in my ears. "Go out there and enjoy yourself," he said. "Do what you always do, do yourself justice, do what I've told you to do. This is the first of many caps."

I did all those things and although we couldn't hang on for a victory it was still a brilliant experience. I was inching my way closer to considering myself a fully-fledged footballer – I finally understood what Olivier was on about.

That first England shirt now belongs to a lady who looked after me, respected me and helped me a lot. I gave it to Karren after signing it. I think she was very touched but I thought it was the least I could do.

In the end, I played 33 games for England Under-21s and felt like an experienced player and also a guy that I like to think the others respected. I had some amazing moments in an England shirt but nothing beats the 2009 UEFA European Under-21 Championship, especially making the final.

Playing in the Under-21 side is different to a Premier League game, which is usually complete chaos. Different players from different sides bring their own qualities to the team and you have to try and gel and adjust to all these new styles.

In 2009 our team was in cruise control. We were so good and it was a wicked experience. I had become a regular by the end of the qualifiers and the way we played suited my game.

Everything about tournament football is great. Getting a letter to your house; going out to have a suit fitted; meeting up with the guys.

It wasn't an emotional moment but I had watched the 2007 tournament and this was something I wanted to get involved with, something to aim for.

We met up in London after a week's break at the end of the Premier League season and the guys gelled so quickly. The aim was to go one place better than the previous tournament. Just one place further. Stuart demanded so much from us and we repaid him even if our hearts were broken by the end. Stuart is a nice guy and he works for the country because he is a legend. It is not an easy job but he had everyone's respect. When he speaks you listen. He will let you know if you step out of line.

Maybe one legacy of Stuart's own time with England is that we would practise penalties every single day.

Every. Single. Day.

I tell you, before we even got in the championship he knew we would need those skills one day so we practised every day. And everybody had to take one, nobody could hide.

In the 2007 championships England had lost to Holland 13-12 on penalties and Stuart was determined that would not happen again. Not on his watch.

During the tournament we played so, so well. We beat Finland in our first game thanks to goals from Lee Cattermole and Micah Richards before we then destroyed Spain in the second match. We were incredible that day. Everyone would think that Spain's youngsters would be brilliant because of the way their full national team were playing and, although they were a good side, we just totally outplayed them. Goals from Fraizer Campbell and James Milner helped us to the win but it could easily have been 4-0 or maybe more. We dominated them physically and threw our weight around a bit.

In that side we had players like Micah Richards, Nedum Onuoha, Lee Cattermole, Mark Noble, Gabriel Agbonlahor and Theo Walcott. Plus we had Joe Hart in goal who was in tremendous form at the time. That is the make-up of a good Premier League side; that team would beat a lot of sides in the top division now.

By the time we got to the semi-final against Sweden we were on a total roll and convinced we could win the tournament. We could defend, we could counter-attack, we could do anything we wanted to. I used to just sit back and let Lee and Mark pour forward.

Sweden were the hosts, it was a big stadium and they were also very confident. But we were convinced we would win it. The pre-match atmosphere was incredible as Gabriel ran the jukebox in the dressing room. Everyone was buzzing while Stuart circled around motivating the guys. "Remember who we are," he stated. "Remember what we stand for. Nobody is leaving here empty-handed." The changing room responded to him instantly and as we walked on to the pitch you could feel the atmosphere and the tension.

I stood there singing the anthem as loud as I could and I just felt total pride. Pride in England, pride in myself for where I was in life and also where I'd come from.

All you could hear early on in the game was Joe shouting at us. Do this, do that, do everything. He ran our defence so well and before you knew it we were 3-0 up. In a European Championship semi-final! We were in dreamland and maybe got a bit casual as they slowly started to peg us back. Before you knew it, we finished normal time at 3-3. We couldn't believe we had thrown away such a lead but Stuart kept us focused and reminded us that we were fit enough to survive extra-time. In the end though Fraizer's dismissal meant we were the side hanging on for penalties, not them, once the 30 minutes was up.

With a few minutes to go, Stuart took me off. It was a bit of a relief to be honest. I won't lie, I didn't want to miss a penalty, I didn't want to be the man responsible if that is how we went out. Stuart praised my performance before I slipped into a tracksuit and had to watch, the same as everybody else.

A penalty shoot-out is a tough experience to go through. James Milner missed our first effort but then they missed theirs as well. All that spot-kick training finally kicked in and we nailed five in a row to win 5-4 in sudden death and book our place in the final. It was all so crazy and the most thrilling feeling ever. We all hugged and mobbed each other before going to a restaurant for a treat. No beer was allowed – which was right – but we gobbled pizza up and celebrated a great victory. We were almost there.

Before the final against Germany – who had beaten Italy in the other last-four game – the dressing room was again buzzing and bubbling. An evening kick-off meant we relaxed all day.

We walked around the pitch before returning to get ready to a special soundtrack of good luck messages which really helped. I remember hearing Trevor Brooking and David Beckham's the most, telling us we had done well to get that far and don't fail now – bring the trophy back with us.

I was sat next to Michael Mancienne ahead of the biggest game of my life and as I slowly got ready I was thinking we could do it. Stuart repeated his own wish to see us lift the trophy and we all thought it was our time. I was in my war mindset by now – let's go and grab it.

Unfortunately it wasn't meant to be.

Germany were just so well equipped. The game meant so much to us but it was so weird. We missed early chances and after that they bossed the game. We didn't expect that because our side was full of Premier League players. But lads like Mesut Ozil, Sebastian Boenisch, Jerome Boateng and Manuel Neuer were all brilliant for them. They showed up when it mattered and that was the difference. In the end, we were hammered 4-0 as Gonzalo Castro, Ozil and Sandro Wagner (twice) showed us who was boss. Looking back, perhaps we thought we had it won before the game started. In my head I was thinking 'this is a piece of cake' and maybe we took Germany too lightly. It still hurts today. With that team we should have won it and we had nothing to show for our efforts.

I was substituted with about 10 minutes to go. After the final whistle I just sat on the grass thinking about what could've been. We had pride in getting to the final but if you don't win then what's the point? Football is about winning, it's as simple as that, and it didn't happen for us.

The dressing room afterwards was so downbeat. We were all so upset and although Stuart tried to lift us, it wasn't going to happen in a million years. We just all sat there shocked and stunned and in silence. Stuart shook our hands but nothing helped. Even ringing dad and praying with him did nothing for me. It was an amazing experience that should have ended in a fairytale but ended in disaster. I just wanted to get home so quickly, hide from everybody and let all the disappointment die down.

I also represented England at the 2011 tournament but that didn't live up to the same hype or have the same feeling or aura around it. It was different because I was hoping to be more involved on the pitch but I didn't play as much and that affects your judgement on how a tournament feels.

Again I got the letter from England and all the other great perks but this time I was to be disappointed when I didn't feature as part of Stuart's main plans.

We met up for about 10 days before we embarked for the tournament in Denmark and we trained hard and enjoyed ourselves. I was ready to offer everything I had but I got a rude awakening when Stuart came to my room on the day of the opening game against Spain. He knocked on the door, walked in and hit me with the bad news.

"I know you're disappointed, you've always been a great example to the other lads but you won't be starting," he said.

He fronted up and gave the news to me straight and I have to give Stuart credit for that. He treated me like a man and just came out with it. Managers make decisions for their own reasons and you've got to respect that, even though I wanted to jump on the first plane back to England. I spoke to dad and he said "do what Stuart tells you, support the team and be professional" and Shauna said exactly the same. "Grind it out," she said. "Support the guys who are around you just like they support you."

We drew against Spain and Ukraine and it meant that we had to win against the Czech Republic. I started the game and was determined to show that I belonged in the starting XI. I had kept my mouth shut about my frustrations, I had worked hard in training and I had stayed in touch with dad and Shauna. This was my time to show everyone.

Unfortunately it wasn't meant to be as we went down 2-1 to go out. Danny Welbeck gave us the lead with a header and we thought we had it in the bag. It goes to show you what we knew. They scored two late goals and we went out. Two years previously we had made the final and now we were going home early. It was my last game for the Under-21s so to go out in that manner left me heartbroken. It was just so hard to take.

After the game the dressing room was like a library. Nothing could be done to cheer us up. Stuart was brilliant, he gathered us together, looked us in the eye and said: "This is tournament football, this is what happens at the sharp end. Learn from this experience."

We dragged ourselves back to the hotel in silence and when it came to departing and checking out I got a phone call from Stuart just before I left my room.

"Come to my room please," he said. I went up to see him and he was great.

"I know you're disappointed." he said. "But you could see what I was trying to do for the team. I know you've been very supportive of the team over the years. Thanks for your efforts."

We shook hands and I left. There were no hard feelings then and there are no hard feelings now. I loved every minute of my Under-21s time – even the difficult moments. It was a huge honour. England had given me this chance to survive and thrive – it was mind-blowing that this kid from Africa was playing in international tournaments – and I will never be able to repay all those responsible for that, starting with Stuart himself.

When I look back on my time with the Under-21s I think it gave me half a chance of playing full internationals. My hope was to get there one day – but God had other plans.

#####

Owen puts his hands on the physio table and wonders what he can possibly say to make it all ok.

He looks at my team-mates sitting down in front of him. Every single one of them refuses to look him in the eye. Socks are rolled down, boots and shinpads are lying everywhere. Not a sound is being made. Grown men, used to vicious banter and not much else, are sat around crying. All of them. Owen can tell they feel a bit embarrassed.

"Listen, this is where we are," he says. "Fabrice is in the best hands. They've given him some shocks and when I know anything you'll know the same. And if you believe in God – start saying your prayers."

He looks at Kevin Davies, our leader, who is sat directly in front of him, choking back tears. "Skipper," Owen says. "Get your tracksuit on. We're going to the hospital right now."

Dr Sam Mohiddin is about to miss his girlfriend Laura-Ann's birthday celebrations. He receives a call from an old friend he trained with who now works at North Middlesex who is intrigued about where I'm going to be heading. Dr Mohiddin has no clue about what has happened at White Hart Lane so he calls the London Chest Hospital and finds out that someone is on their way. He jumps into his car and heads to work from his home in Hackney.

On the ambulance every person's role has become clearer without a word of instruction being uttered.

Not one.

These blokes are psychic. Dr Tobin works my chest, Peter keeps his eye on the oxygen while Paul and Dr Deaner sort out the drugs I need to come back.

The only person letting the side down is me.

#9

Love And Hope

AN ambulance is not a steady place when it comes to trying to save someone's life. As Dr Tobin presses down on my chest he cannot quite get a full compression in. He's all over the place because the football boots he's still got on are causing him to slip and slide all over the ambulance's floor. It's like trying to perform CPR on a surfboard.

"Here, let me help," Anthony says and he jams himself against a seat behind Dr Tobin, holding him securely and anchoring him in place, stopping the slipping instantly. Problem solved.

I've had 10 shocks by now but still nothing. Dr Deaner glances at Dr Tobin and offers a look that says all it needs to about how concerned he is getting.

'A 23-year-old professional athlete should be back by now,' he thinks to himself. If I was going to survive then Dr Deaner reckons the pitch was the likeliest place for that to happen.

But we're not on the pitch. We're in an ambulance and I'm lying here doing nothing at all.

More adrenaline, more nothing. One thing seems to lead to another in this cramped, sweaty space.

The line Dr Deaner has placed in my leg won't stay in place. Blood spurts from my groin as it becomes clear that it's come loose. I wish I could lean down and help out. My elasticated Bolton shorts won't stay out of the way, they keep falling down and snagging the line. It's not the end of the world but another procedure that needs to be repeated.

Dr Deaner aims for the other side of my groin this time and easily makes it two from two for the day. But my shorts continue to get on his nerves. "Pass me those scissors Pete," he says. Peter passes them over and my shorts go the same way as my shirt did. That's the end of that.

"Stay where you are, I'll be there as soon as I can," Ricardo Gardner's partner, Suki, shouts down the phone to Shauna before racing down to Cheshire from their place in Bolton. The four of us have become really good mates and regularly go out together. After Warwick, Suki is the first person Shauna rings. She needs her calm advice. She's like Shauna's big sister. She knows Suki won't collapse on her. Shauna can't let anything distract her from her mission of getting to London as soon as possible.

"Right guys, let's move the pads back and front," Dr Deaner says to Dr Tobin and Peter. Up until now the AED pads have been stuck on my chest. But they ain't been doing much. Dr

Deaner decides it's time to roll the dice.

Dr Tobin stands aside for a split second and is starting to think that whatever they try is going to be too little too late. He's not a pessimistic man, just a realistic one. If a 23-year-old isn't alive and kicking after 13 shocks and a ton of drugs then his medical experience tells him that my odds are getting worse by the second.

Peter wouldn't normally change the position of the pads, leaving that to those who specialise in heart trouble, those who work in a secure hospital rather than on the back of a rocking ambulance that is threading its way through London.

Well, today, that specialist isn't on the end of a phone or a mile away waiting for me to turn up. He's stood next to him.

'Let's give it a go,' Peter thinks. 'Let's do everything we can for this guy.'

"Ready, brace, roll," he says. I'm tipped to my right as one pad is placed on my back and a new one is stuck on my front. Dr Deaner also hooks me up to the ambulance's own defibrillator rather than the one used on the pitch. He's scared the battery might be starting to fade. After 13 massive shocks it's a good call to make.

#####

I first met Shauna in a nightclub called Oceana in Birmingham. It's not hard to remember when it was because we'd won our first home game in the Premier League that day! That might not be the most romantic way of remembering when it was but beating Bolton Wanderers – of all teams – and then meeting her means September 15, 2007 is an extra special date in my mind.

After the victory I was seriously pumped up and ready for a big night out. Olivier Kapo mentioned that some of the guys wanted to check out this new club so I was more than happy to go along. Myself, Radhi Jaïdi, Bruno N'Gotty, Mehdi Nafti and Kapo all piled into the place where we went in the VIP room and started enjoying ourselves.

It was then that I saw her.

The VIP area had windows which meant you could see out but people couldn't see in and I spotted this girl, surrounded by her friends, having a great time.

"Olivier, I'm going out there," I said. "I've got to speak to that girl." To this day I don't know where the courage or will to do it came from. I was normally very, very shy when it came to speaking to girls. But it just felt like something I had to do so I found this boldness from somewhere. It took some bravery to go over and I wasn't even drinking so I couldn't even blame that!

Olivier soon started grinning and knew what I was playing at. You know what mates are like – he tried to ruin it from the start. "Stay in here," he said. "There's plenty of girls around here. Be quiet, man."

But my mind was made up. "You guys can do what you want – you can stay in here forever – but I'm going out there," I said, not quite sure what I was going to do or say when I finally got over to Shauna.

"Hi, do you girls want a drink," I nervously said. Looking back now I could cringe at what I was wearing – boy, I was loud back then! I managed to make some Gucci shoes, jeans and a shirt look like the worst outfit you've ever seen. I was certainly looking worse than Shauna, put it like that.

"No, we're ok thanks," was the answer I heard back above the sound of the speakers. It looked like I was heading for disaster but Shauna's mates then rescued me by saying "yeah, ok, we'll have a drink." I've never been so relieved to have to buy a few rounds.

That bought me some time with Shauna and we slowly started talking and smiling more, her looking gorgeous, me trying not to ruin it. We ended up dancing and I kept sorting out drinks for her and her mates and before I knew it the guys had left and it was time for the club to close.

I knew it was getting close to crunch time but because I was driving I offered to give Shauna and her friends a lift back to their homes. Of course I left Shauna until last, getting increasingly nervous as the number of people in my car dropped from five, to four, to three until there was eventually just two of us left.

This was it. I turned to her in the car and said "when can I see you again?" We then swapped numbers and I tried to remain calm despite the big problems on the horizon.

Firstly I'd told her I was 24 when I was only 18 and, secondly, I'd told her that my name was... erm... Marcus.

Back then it just seemed easier to give a stupid false name so you didn't attract the wrong girls who only seemed interested in you because of your day job. There's no denying that a lot of girls only show you any attention because you're a footballer. By pretending to be someone else, I at least got a chance to work out whether a girl was for real or not.

The problems didn't end there either. After we had swapped numbers I took a deep breath, turned to my left and tried to give her a kiss on the lips. All I got back was cheek – and I mean that literally. There would be no late-night kiss tonight and I was actually ok with that and impressed with that. This girl seemed to be the real deal and still seemed to be in control and not turning crazy on me. I happily dropped her off and drove home excitedly, thinking that I'd found a great girl who liked me for me and me alone. I soon realised that she was also as sharp and as tuned in as it gets.

"What do you do for a living?"

Those were the first words I heard when I answered the phone in bed at the crack of dawn the next day.

Shauna had gone home and immediately worked out that I wasn't who I said I was.

"I don't know any guy in Birmingham driving an Audi A3 and buying drinks for people all night," she said. "So come clean, are you that Fabrice guy who plays football?"

Oh shit. She had seen my photo in the paper.

"Let me call you back," I spluttered before putting the phone down and cursing myself for being so stupid. It looked like I'd ruined it from the start. I told you I was useless with girls.

I ended up speeding over to her place to try and undo the damage from the night before. I took her to Nando's near Broad Street – classy hey? – I laid it on the line and told her what was up and we had a conversation about who I was.

I introduced myself properly as Fabrice and she certainly put me in my place and told me she wasn't impressed by me being a footballer. Soon after, over a plate of chicken wings, I finally managed to clarify everything and we sorted it out and I apologised.

I was in the doghouse so I picked the bill up and I knew I had to do everything right, which finally worked, and we became very close very quickly. We just clicked immediately – you know how it is when you find the right person.

She used to live about 20 minutes from my place and I would

drive over and see her about four times a week. She then passed her driving test so she would come around to mine as well. We just did couple stuff like going to the cinema or a nice restaurant.

Shauna basically started kicking me into shape. And I needed it. I had lived at home before moving to Birmingham and was no different to any other lazy teenage boy. When I moved north, firstly into a flat and then my house in Solihull, the place was like a normal single man's pad – a bit of a mess. But Shauna soon changed all that. She came round, showed off her amazing cooking skills and even cleaned my clothes and helped sort me out. I was thinking 'this is getting serious' as she brought some order and shape to my life. My step-mum had been the only other person who had taken care of that kind of stuff but now Shauna was pulling me into gear as well. She was just a wonderful, nice girl – a very special woman. She came over one night with the ingredients for rice, peas and chicken and cooked me my first proper meal in ages. Wow. I have nothing but love for that woman. She is very, very special for a million reasons. She gave me Joshua, who is the greatest gift in the world. She is strong, confident and always speaks her mind and, there's no two ways about it, she puts me in my place when I need it.

The power of a woman when it comes to making a home and a family cannot be defeated and Shauna is no different. She is an amazing person.

However, that does not mean I was the perfect early boyfriend and I made some mistakes that could have proved to be the end for us as a couple.

During 2007, after me and Shauna had been going out for about nine months and after I had started playing more at Birmingham, I also started playing the field and we inevitably split up. What can I say? I was an idiot; I thought I was a playboy back then.

My earlier lack of confidence with girls had been replaced by me thinking I could run around Birmingham trying to get my groove on. I hold my hands up entirely – it was silly of me to act in that way, it was silly of me to hurt Shauna that way and to also get other people involved.

I wanted the freedom that being a young man can offer you, especially a young man with a high profile. I'm not the first or the last footballer to act stupidly when all these temptations are placed in front of you. I met this other girl at the barbers and got wrapped up in something I shouldn't have done.

The madness didn't end there either.

After leaving Shauna for that girl, I then bounced on to another very quickly, which just made me look like more of an idiot. Shauna was very, very upset. Very. Upset. It was the worst I've ever seen her and it was unforgivable. When I look back I just think I was a young man who was clueless about what matters. I could've handled it very differently.

One day Shauna rang me and said we needed to talk. Although we had split up we remained in touch and she came over to my house and dropped the news on me.

I was going to be a father.

I thought all hell was going to break loose. At the time I was very selfish and all I thought about was me, me, me. Shauna had got pregnant right at the end of our relationship, just before it had ended. She obviously didn't know for a while that she was expecting and then had to put up with me and my behaviour until she came clean and told me the score.

After announcing her news, she told me how it was and told me that I had to be a good father to my baby. At the time I couldn't believe what I had got myself into.

However, I knew it was time to be a man and step up and take responsibility. The selfishness had to end. I had to take care of my child. I'd got myself into this situation so it was time to do the right thing.

After Shauna left, I rang my step-mum Gertrude and told her the situation.

"I think you need to tell your dad in person," she said. I reluctantly agreed despite being nervous about it.

They still thought I was the shy, innocent Fabrice they had sent up to Birmingham but I had changed a fair bit by then and when I drove down to London the next day I didn't know what to say or how to say it.

I psyched myself up in the car outside before almost sneaking in through the front door. Dad was in the living room and my appearance was a surprise. He knew straight away that something wasn't right.

"Dad, I need to talk to you," I said. "I've been seeing a girl in Birmingham and now she's pregnant."

He sat opposite me as he absorbed the news. He wasn't too impressed. I was just a kid really.

"Why, why, why," he said, before adding that I had to do what was right.

I left the house as quick as I could as dad said he needed some time to think about the news. I felt upset and I felt we could've had a decent chat but maybe it's just African culture not to talk about such things straight away.

I rang him when I got back to Birmingham that night and we were ok, we smoothed any bumps over and I can hardly blame him. He was right, it was all a mess.

I soon got advice from others such as Rashid who told me what I already knew – that is was time to be a man, be a father, be a decent human being.

Warwick said the same thing and I knew I would stand by Shauna when she had our child.

I remained with the other girl throughout this time because I couldn't find the courage to tell her I had got another girl pregnant but I rented Shauna an apartment and provided her with everything she needed.

Just to complicate matters further, I made my switch to Bolton during the summer of 2008 and the complications followed me even further north. I was trying to get on and succeed at the new club as well as sorting my private life out.

When I moved to Bolton I still hadn't split up with the other girl while still trying to provide for Shauna. What can I say? I was a fool and I would do a lot of things differently these days.

Inevitably she found out about Shauna's pregnancy and she was really upset. She arrived at my place in Knutsford and I had to tell her everything. She had every right to know that I was going to become a father and that Shauna was the mother. It wasn't a pretty conversation. All I seemed to do was cause trouble to people I cared about. It wasn't and isn't a proud time in my life.

We remained together all the way through the pregnancy while I still tried to support Shauna as much as I could. It was a case of juggling my life by standing by my responsibilities as well as staying in another relationship.

Finally I got a phone call on a Friday night and it was Shauna saying "I might give birth at any time now." I stayed in the northwest to go training on the Saturday and when I came back it was clear the labour had started after one of Shauna's mates rang me and told me to get to Birmingham as soon as possible.

How many times can you see your first child born? Exactly. It was hardly something I wanted to miss, plus my first child might be my last.

I raced to Birmingham and she was in the waiting room with her mum, Marva, who was understandably frosty with me. She was taken into the delivery room and I went in with her and it was all done very quickly. I kept telling her to push and she was screaming her head off. I was holding her hand and I thought she was going to crush my fingers! I guess she was in more pain than me though…

Anyway, in no time at all I was handed this tiny little bundle.

And it was at that split second on Saturday, November 1, 2008 that I became a man.

I held him as he cried – this tiny, perfect healthy baby boy. I was buzzing. In fact I was miles beyond buzzing.

#####

"Is he dead?" Shauna asks Dean Brooke, the Bolton player liaison officer who has just got in touch.

"I don't want to say, I don't know. They're doing everything they can," he replies. "We can send a car to come and get you," he adds. Forget that. It will take too long. Shauna's mum takes care of Joshua, as well as rushing Shauna and Suki to Wilmslow train station.

The two of them stand in the waiting room desperately hoping there is a train to London. There isn't a train to London.

As they stand there Shauna looks up at the TV screen and

watches BBC News. The screen is covered in pictures of me. They are pictures of me dying.

> *'Fabrice Muamba, who plays football for Bolton Wanderers, has collapsed during an FA Cup match against Tottenham Hotspur,' the newsreader announces. 'We will bring you more news on this breaking story when we get it.'*

Shauna is calm and cool. She's on auto-pilot. Finally her and Suki manage to get a train to Stockport where they then jump on board and head for Euston. They upgrade to First Class. It only costs an extra £15 on a Saturday.

She closes her eyes and wishes she could be in London with me, right now. She doesn't know what she should be expecting or what she should be thinking.

Nobody does.

#10

Buying Time

AFTER Birmingham had been relegated I went to New York that summer. While I was there, Warwick called me to let me know that Bolton Wanderers were interested in me. Their manager wanted to meet, so when I got back, we drove up to the Reebok Stadium where Gary Megson outlined his plans. He wanted to build a young side and he invited me to be part of it.

I cost five and a bit million and my wage also increased substantially. I'm living the dream here. £5,000 appearance fee, £5,000 win bonus. That kind of money was so far beyond my understanding at the time it might as well have been dollars or euros or whatever. I couldn't get my head around it, although I did like to spend a fair bit on a nice watch and stuff like that. I also moved in to a tidy apartment above a bookshop. It was great, life was different up north and I used to enjoy going out in Manchester. I kept checking Birmingham's results. They had made me very welcome, I owed them so much and they were really good to me. I still check their results now.

Gary was a good manager and I respect him for bringing me to Bolton. Some managers like to raise their voice and some don't. Gary did. He really did. That was just the way he was. There is nothing wrong with that.

People often wonder now whether managers are as feared as they once were because players are on so much more money than ever before. But, trust me, there is always respect. They are the boss and they can do what they want. He was very tough on me, like so many before him had been, but again that was only because he wanted the best for me and he was so desperate for Bolton to succeed. I was not cheap and like any manager he wanted me to reward his faith. I tried my best to do that.

I remember one day he tore into me at half-time when we were playing at home. We were in the dressing room and he fired up, rolling the cuffs up on his shirt, which he always did when he got angry. I didn't think he was going to punch me, that's just what he did. He just went mental. Effing and blinding and calling me all sorts of names. He just blew it.

I just kept my mouth shut because he is the manager, so you have to take it but in my head I was saying 'this man is talking so much rubbish, he best keep quiet'. He is the man in charge. But the clock was ticking and I was thinking 'if he doesn't shut up, I'm going to punch him'. It went on and on. 'God help me,' I said to myself, 'this man is pushing the boundaries, I would like to see him try and hit me – let's see who wins'.

I obviously never would've done but every player at some point has thought the same thing. If they say they haven't then they're lying. Thinking something and doing something are two separate things though and I had no problems with his approach. He's got more experience in the game than me so who was I to argue?

Gary used to love a shout but he would back down if somebody gave it to him in return. Kevin Nolan was one who used to scream back just as loud as Gary when he felt it was justified. It was a noisy and opinionated dressing room full of big characters.

One of the biggest I've met is El-Hadji Diouf. Boy that man can play. He is a serious player – but also a nutcase! I first met him at the training ground. I stuck out my hand and introduced myself and he just grinned, dressed in his loud clothes with a massive gold chain dangling off him. "El-Hadji Diouf," he said, "the best player in the team." I remember thinking: 'why would you say that?' but he backed it up on the training ground. He never gave the ball away. I've seen a lot of good players but he is different. "I'm the best player on this pitch," he used to shout when we were training. The other guys used to roll their eyes and say "it's just Dioufy!"

Me and Ricardo Gardner also became very good mates quite quickly. He was a very loyal Bolton player. Ricardo used to play Jamaican music all the time and I loved that stuff, so we bonded.

I joined Bolton at the same time as Johan Elmander. He cost about £11m from Toulouse and was immediately under pressure because of the transfer fee. He had vision, energy and desire to burn but the goals just wouldn't come for him at first, although that changed later on.

Bolton's side was full of men who wanted to do well for the team. Matty Taylor was a good talker on the pitch, constantly telling me where I should be, while Gary Cahill was like me, quiet, but he led by example. I hope he gets to captain England one day.

They were all really good lads and they also knew how to have a good time, which is so important in building team spirit.

It was never anything too crazy but team nights out were always fun. We used to go out in Manchester and Kev would be the leader. If we had a few days off and we could go for a beer we would do.

One Christmas we went to Dublin for a party. It was a great, different experience. We flew from Manchester on a Saturday, the whole squad, stayed in the city centre and then flew back on a Monday. That's about the only thing I can remember, the rest is a blur!

We had a great time. My only one hazy memory is that I had my first – and last – pint of Guinness. We were in a pub and Jlloyd Samuel walked over, grinning, and said: "Come on, you have to drink it." I don't drink much anyway and, oh my God, what is that stuff? I've never tried it since and I won't be doing so either. It has nothing good about it! They won't be sponsoring me in the future, that's for sure. I like Malibu and coke and drinks like that. On that trip we certainly had a few.

God, I was rough when we got back. We didn't have to return to training until the Wednesday as the gaffer decided to give us another day to recover – and we needed it. I lay in bed for two days, sleeping and drinking as much water as I could. I needed to get myself together. I crawled to McDonald's for some large fries before going back to bed. It was a funny experience but a one-off. We knew when we had to put in the hard work and were extremely disciplined at the right times.

One of my favourite memories at Bolton is when Joshua was

born. Bolton were playing so I couldn't hang around too long at the hospital in Birmingham. The next day I drove to the Reebok as high as a kite and told the guys what had happened.

Kevin Nolan, Ricardo Gardner, Andy O'Brien and Kevin Davies all knew what was going on and how complicated everything was but at that moment in time the only thing that mattered was that I was a dad. Big smiles and big handshakes were the order of the day.

"Make sure you do well for the little man," Kevin Nolan said, with a big grin on his face and we certainly did that. On the pitch that afternoon I felt I was three times the man I had been, especially as we beat Manchester City 2-0!

#####

The change in pad position works. Kind of. My heart starts firing again but not in a good way.

I've got a ventricular tachycardia, which is a clever way of saying it's beating way too fast; so fast in fact that it looks as if it's just twitching and shuddering because it's banging so quickly. That is not really any better than where I was before because although my heart is going it's still not doing anything to pump blood around my body.

A fast heart rate doesn't mean anything unless your heart pumps blood at the same time.

Mine isn't. From a medical point of view I might as well still be on the pitch. All this concern, all this amazing hard work, all the prayers I'm already receiving.

All of it is going to waste.

All the guys around me know I'm slipping away.

All of Britain has started praying for me.
All of me inches towards the end.

#####

When Kevin Nolan spoke, we listened. Kevin's attitude was that he was always our leader. He was so determined to succeed and set a great example. As a young player you need a guy who will speak to you like that. When I went to Bolton I realised this was a different ball game. The whole structure of the club, the way it was run, the demands of me in games and in training: I knew it was time to step up and Kevin helped me do that.

That's why we were all shocked when he was sold to Newcastle United. We had lost a big character and our captain.

It all happened so quickly. It was January, 2009. We went to training one morning and Kevin left pretty swiftly but I didn't think much of it.

When I got home, I dropped my car keys on the table, turned on Sky Sports News and it was announcing that he had gone. He might have said something to the other guys but he said nothing to me. I tried to call him but couldn't get hold of him, although he sent me a text saying 'it was for football reasons'.

I was just a young player and I didn't know what was going on upstairs, so I was confused. Why were we selling our captain? The other players felt the same.

When Kevin Nolan left, Kevin Davies became the main leader. They are two different characters. Nolan is outspoken and bubbly and will always speak his mind and although Davies does that as well he is bit quieter. He prefers to lead by example, which he has always done. The man is a Bolton legend.

#####

Owen and Kevin sit in the back seat of a marked police car, quietly impressed at how quickly they're getting across London. The lights are on and the guy in the front is flying. The two of them left the dressing room and Owen grabbed the most senior officer he could find and told him that he needed to go wherever I was going.

The officer does a wonderful job in rustling up a car in no time at all and Owen curses himself for not getting his name so he can thank him later. Because the stadium is emptying, the car cannot pull up to the front of White Hart Lane so the gaffer and Kevin walk out of the entrance and round to the side. They try and squeeze their way through the crowd and it doesn't take long before they're inevitably spotted by stunned Spurs fans leaving in silence.

As Owen and Kevin approach their ride, all they can hear is hundreds of fans shouting to them. "Good luck," says one. "We're praying for you," goes another.

And Owen is again struck by how amazing football fans can be when it really matters.

#####

After finishing 13th in the 2008-09 season, we made a reasonable start to the new campaign, only narrowly losing to Manchester United and Liverpool. Then, at the end of October, we started to go downhill. We really struggled.

I began to think Gary's days were numbered just after Christmas when we drew 2-2 against Hull City at home after being 2-0 up. We got booed off the park that night and that is a horrible feeling. The dressing room afterwards was not a good place.

The lads were so down. As I walked off I knew that something was going to happen. Sure enough, the day after the Hull game, the club made the announcement that Gary was leaving.

Ultimately, Gary left because we just couldn't fire as a team. We had no consistency. When you are doing badly and fighting relegation, you are just always under pressure. You can never escape from it – it's in your head every waking moment. The media scrutiny is always there.

I didn't hear it personally that he had gone. Two mates tried to message my Blackberry asking me if he had left and I didn't know – it turns out they knew before I did. I then chased it up and found out. Players should be informed about these things but, again, we're just employees so a club can do what they want. You often don't get much information as a player. Play football and behave yourself, they're the only rules.

When a manager leaves a club it makes life very strange for a while. It's like a car that's lost its driver. And what happens if your car's not got a driver? It crashes. Plus, when you are training and there is no gaffer then everyone slackens a little bit. I don't care what anyone says, you don't train as hard when you know there's no manager around to keep you in line. It was different in many ways – training was good but not as strict as it would have been if Gary was there.

The whole club started wondering what the next move was. We would sit in training and think: 'What is happening, who is going to lead the club?' The players didn't know what was going on. I used to go home after training and wonder who was going to replace Gary but I didn't think it was my place to go and knock on

Mr Gartside's door and ask him. Football doesn't work like that.

We started to hear the rumours about Owen Coyle coming in because of the job he had done at Burnley and it helped that he was a former Bolton player. He did a very good job at Burnley, who had just been promoted to the Premier League and he was appointed in January, 2010.

When he arrived, he came into the Reebok dressing room looking sharp in a suit. He was very positive and bubbly. He shook all our hands and went around the dressing room introducing himself. He knew all our names, which was impressive. Some of the guys' names I struggled to remember, never mind the new boss! He elaborated on his plans for the future and where he wanted the football club to go. He said he wanted us to be free flowing and more positive on the pitch.

Owen is a man who misses football, misses being out on the pitch and playing 90 minutes every weekend. He used to love taking part in training. It's very much his style to get involved with his players and he was unlike any other manager I've known in that way. Arsene used to let us get on with it; Steve only got involved in the Young v Old match on a Friday; Alex loved tactics but wouldn't really play and Gary didn't much either. Owen was far different but although he would act like one of the boys at times, we all understood the boundaries. We respected him and he was our manager, not our friend.

We picked up a few more wins with Owen in charge and ended up finishing 14th in 2009-10. At the end of the season I signed a four-year extension. I had had a clause in my earlier contract that stated if I played 50 games for the first team it would trigger a new deal. I got to that landmark, the club were happy with me and I was happy with them. I was feeling like a Premier League player by now – it felt like the stage I belonged on. I knew I'd played well and deserved the new deal.

#####

The ambulance begins to beep and slow down as it reverses into place. I've arrived at the London Chest Hospital.

"We need to disconnect everything slowly and properly," Peter says. It was pointless rushing me onto the ambulance and it's just as pointless now rushing me off.

The defibrillator is taken off the wall and the drip in my groin is carefully removed from the ambulance ceiling by Dr Deaner as Anthony and Dr Tobin continue to perform CPR while Peter keeps the oxygen coming. The back doors fly open and Zoe Astrolakis, the registrar working at the time, looks up and sees Dr Deaner. The two know each other well.

"Are you alright?" she says. "Do you need a hug?" Just because these people do this every day doesn't mean they're robots.

Dr Deaner went to a football match to catch up with his brothers and watch his team win. Now he's in an ambulance trying to save my life. Who can blame Zoe for worrying about him? For all he knows his bike is still attached to the railings outside White Hart Lane, although he hopes Dr Hogan has managed to get a message to his brothers to shift it.

Up until now I've been in Peter, Dr Tobin and Anthony's world. Now I move into Dr Deaner's.

I'm lifted off the ambulance trolley and onto a hospital bed. In that split-second the baton is passed on. My fate now rests in the hands of those inside.

I fly up a ramp straight down a corridor 15 metres long, I turn right into the cath lab area before taking another left into the lab itself.

Peter is still the main man when it comes to oxygen and he talks with an anaesthetist about my airway before handing over. His night's work is done.

He walks off to a viewing area with Barbara, Paul and Anthony to watch others doing what he's been doing.

Trying to save my life.

#11

On The Brink

SHAUNA looks out of the window of the train as Suki does what all good mates do.

"Let's stay positive," she says. "We don't know what is happening. He'll be ok."

Dean Brooke rings back. "Where should we head to?" Shauna asks. Dean isn't sure. The North Middlesex seems like the closest hospital but he's heard that I'm heading elsewhere.

Shauna looks out of the window again and begins to pray. 'Just be alive', she says to herself. 'I don't care what state he's in. If he's alive then we've got something to work with.'

Dr Tobin decides to stay in the cath lab itself, standing well back and out of the way. He's still got his studs on as well as his official matchday kit. He has grassy knees and muddy boots. He is guided to a seat in the corner and begins to watch and all he can think is 'I'm going to get thrown out for the state of my clothes.'

The cath lab is rammed full of x-ray equipment, ultrasound, nurses, anaesthetists, electrophysiologists and experts of all shapes and sizes. The NHS is throwing the best they've got at me.

I hope I can repay them.

Dr Deaner races off to put some theatre blues on, comes back and immediately gets to work.

"Let's get a better line in," is his first call and a sub-clavian line is inserted under my left collarbone. This immediately improves my chances of coming back. The bigger and better the line inserted, the quicker they can get drugs into me.

An auto-pulse is placed over my chest, sitting snugly against me, and someone flicks the switch. Manual CPR is knackering and I've had it for almost 50 minutes. It's time to let the machine take the strain when it comes to compressing my chest. Nothing can beat your own heart and lungs but mine are nowhere to be seen right now. The auto-pulse plus the oxygen I'm receiving are doing their best to con my body into thinking I'm ok. But my body isn't stupid.

All these guys are doing is buying me time. And they're running out of money.

Dr Tobin walks outside and the scale of what's happening hits him. I'm his mate and I'm dying in front of him.

He stands against a wall in the corridor and begins to cry, sliding down the wall until he sits on the cold floor. This is all too much.

#####

In 2010-11 we got off to a great start and I expected big things from us. Owen had repaired a lot of damage and kept us up comfortably the year before. A decent away win early on against West Ham United gave us all a boost. I was playing well, developing nicely and enjoying it. The players seemed to click and we were all buzzing. We wanted to do far better than the season before. We knew we could defend, we played without fear and felt we had some strength in depth.

We achieved some good results during the course of the campaign, drawing with Manchester United and beating my old team Arsenal but in the end we could only finish 14th again, which was a real shame.

We did manage to get to the FA Cup semi-final, but ended up losing 5-0 to Stoke on a disastrous day. Our form tailed off and although we lost our remaining five games in a drab finish to the season, I was still relatively happy at the Reebok.

In the summer of 2011, I decided to work harder than ever to get myself in shape for the season ahead. I was in New York three weeks before pre-season started but rather than taking in the sights and the sounds I spent most of the time with a personal trainer, pushing myself.

When I came back from America I was by far and away in the best condition ever. That gave me a massive mental boost. Football is a very competitive game and you want to always be the best you can. Always. I knew that when I went into pre-season I wanted to feel ready. Weights, cardio, interval training – I did it all and gave it my all. Nothing else was good enough.

When it comes to physical fitness, a lot of players now spend their summers trying to get in condition before pre-season is even on the horizon. Some only give themselves a week's headstart but a lot of others like to be dedicated all year round. That's just the way the game has developed. You have to be in peak condition to play in the Premier League or you will be found out quickly and you don't get there without sacrificing certain things. If you have a day off from training and spend it drinking beer there is always someone somewhere working hard in the gym, sipping water. And when you come back after your holidays, you have to make sure you're not off the pace. It's about giving off a good vibe to the manager and I felt I had done that.

That great pre-season reaped instant rewards as I scored against QPR in the opening match. I was really excited about our chances of doing well in the season ahead.

#####

Owen gets out of the police car and presses the green button on his Nokia 9210. The phone is ancient but it's got so many numbers on it he doesn't want to replace it. He normally has it on silent but as the hospital looms into sight he turns up the volume in case someone wants to get in touch about Fabrice.

A minute later it rings. "Owen, it's Kenny," says a voice at the other end. It's Kenny Dalglish, the Liverpool manager. They have a game against Stoke City in one of the other FA Cup quarter-finals tomorrow. "I'll say this quickly; we're all thinking about Fabrice and the club. Can you please pass on our best. If you need anything at all let me know."

By the end of the day almost every club in the country has got in touch to offer whatever help Bolton need.

Players, too, across the country are taking to their mobiles to show their support. Justin Hoyte tweets: 'He has been there for me since we was little and I cannot imagine life without such a great guy! Love him to bits' and Johan Djourou taps: 'Love you so much man! Keep fighting. Everybody please pray for him he's an amazing man and friend'. Stuart Holden, my Bolton team-mate, also writes a message. 'Praying for you Fab. Hope he's OK. Thoughts with him and his family. For all those asking, I know as much as you do. Waiting anxiously for updates from team-mates. Fab is a fighter!'

It's not just my close mates that are rallying around. Others use Twitter to show their concern...

Frank Lampard: 'We are all Wanderers tonight.'

Kyle Walker: 'Doesn't matter who you support. Doesn't matter if you aren't a football fan. Doesn't matter if you aren't religious. Pray for Fabrice Muamba.'

Rio Ferdinand: 'Come on Fabrice Muamba, praying for you.'

Rafael van der Vaart: 'Terrible what happened with Muamba during the game. We're all praying for him.'

Jack Wilshere: 'Hope Muamba is okay! Thoughts with him.'

David Gold: 'Fabrice Muamba is one of the nicest and most respectful young men I ever met in football. I'm thinking of you Fab, get well soon.'

Wayne Rooney: 'Hope Fabrice Muamba is OK. Praying for him and his family. Still in shock.'

Robin van Persie: 'I'm so sad about what happened to Fabrice Muamba today. Played with him for a couple of years. What a great guy. Always a smile on his face. Please Fabrice bring that smile back. My thoughts are with you and your lovely family!'

There are many more, too many to mention. Fans from clubs across the country are also posting messages on websites wishing me well as I fight for my life.

Owen and Kevin see Dr Tobin straight away and he fills them in on the situation. Dr Tobin is shaken and thinks Owen and Kevin are in shock. They look at him and think the same. It's looking really bad.

Owen asks about Shauna, finds a side room and rings her on the train. "Just tell me he's alive," she says. "Just please tell me he's still alive."

#####

Despite my positive start, my early season optimism didn't last. I started to fall out of favour. We had a lot of midfielders all competing for a place. There was Mark Davies, Darren Pratley, Stuart Holden, Nigel Reo Coker and me all trying to get starting positions. I was in for a week, then out for a week and I started to feel frustrated. I only played five out of our opening 10 matches and felt like I couldn't build up any consistency.

On the Friday, we used to run through the starting XI team shape and if I wasn't involved, it used to drive me mad. Those not picked for the next day's game would break off and work with assistant manager Sandy Stewart. No matter how hard he tried, he couldn't make me feel any better.

"I know you're all disappointed," he would say as we shuffled across to where the reserves trained, "but let's work hard for the team." In my head I would think 'why are you taking me for an idiot? If you don't want me here just say so.'

I would go in to Owen to try and find out why I wasn't getting picked. He would say: "I want to play someone else in front of you, you're not performing to your best." When you hear that once you go away, accept it and come back stronger. But nothing changed and when I went back I got the same message. I would walk away thinking 'he is talking rubbish'. You wonder what else you can do to get back into the team.

I'd go to training and work hard but deep inside I knew I'd be left out again. It made me so moody. I used to drive home thinking 'why aren't I getting picked? What is this guy playing at?' It was on my mind 24 hours a day. I would go through the front door and get mad, shouting at Shauna and just not being in a good place. I wanted to prove myself and I wasn't getting the chance to do that. By the time February came around – just six weeks before my collapse – I decided it was time to go.

"Let's get out of here man," I said one day as Warwick sat on the couch in my living room. "It's time to do something different. I can't take what is happening to me anymore." He knew I wasn't happy and he sat there, sipping his coffee, trying to counsel me through. "Have a look about for me," I said. "If any clubs are interested then let's get moving forward."

I was used to playing week in and week out and those days looked numbered. I spoke to Shauna in the kitchen about an exit plan. I was really down and told her I was tired of not playing. The evidence was there that I should be in the team. The stats seemed to show that when I played we won. I might not be the best player on the pitch but I never stopped trying and what I did for the team was good work. The manager just didn't fancy me at the time and I had to make up my mind about what I wanted to do. I needed to play so badly but it wasn't happening.

The only player I told was Martin Petrov. We were in the dressing room at Euxton one day and I just unloaded the burden. "Martin, I need to get out, I'm getting no game time," I said. "Hang on in there, I know you're young and want to play but your time will come," he responded. His words didn't help much because I was just so frustrated.

Owen had his own opinions. Being a manager is not an easy job – I accept that and it is nothing personal. I just wanted to play football and you can't keep everyone happy, in football and in life. From 35 games a season to a lot less than that is just not something I could handle. I seemed to get the same excuses and it wasn't good enough for me.

People may think I'm being disrespectful and ungrateful to Bolton by outlining my plans to get out of the club despite what they later did for me following my collapse. But I can't help that and I can't lie and pretend that before the cardiac arrest I was all happy and everything was great. Trust me, it wasn't.

Bolton did so much for me after my cardiac arrest and I'm so grateful to the club. So many people have gone above and beyond to help me recover – including Owen. But the truth of the matter is that, for footballing reasons, I was on my way out. I'm a passionate man and it was hurting me not being involved.

Bolton's fans should know that I loved playing for them and that it wasn't anything else other than sheer frustration that was driving me away. I didn't want more money. I just wanted the shirt or if not the shirt then at least a decent excuse for why I didn't have it. I felt, rightly or wrongly, that I wasn't getting any of that.

When I stepped out on that White Hart Lane pitch on that March evening, there were a lot of feelings swirling around in my head. I knew that I had a big point to prove. Perhaps I had one last chance to show the boss that I could be a part of his plans at this club I loved. But there was also a part of me that feared it was all too late.

#####

As Dr Mohiddin arrives on the scene the cath lab is full of slick chaos. Different experts, different specialists, different heroes all working separately but together at the same time.

"We need an echo," Dr Deaner states, asking for an ultrasound of my heart to see what that will show up. I'm being given more amiodarone and also bicarbonate because my blood has become too acidic and that needs to be reversed.

The echo, short for echocardiogram, shows that there's no build-up of fluid around my heart so that problem is ruled out. Those in the cath lab want to tick off, one by one, the problems that could be causing this situation. It's about keeping cool under pressure and working swiftly to rule out one thing after another.

For the third time in less than an hour Dr Deaner hovers over me, ready to prod me with more wires. He wants to inject a contrast dye into my heart to take a picture and see if he and his team can spot whether my arteries are blocked.

He holds onto the side of the trolley as he steadies himself, hitting the perfect spot in my groin, accessing my femoral artery first time. He could probably do this in his sleep these days. He knows he's in the artery because blood spurts out and catches his theatre blues as well as dribbling onto my thigh.

He takes his time, inching a small catheter all the way up to my heart before injecting the dye. In no time at all he gets confirmation of what he thought. There's no blockage. My left and right coronary arteries look as healthy as can be. As I lie in the middle of the room, the only still object in a space full of people, Dr Deaner approaches Dr Tobin and lays it on the line. It's two professionals looking at my situation clinically. "If things don't start to change soon we're getting to the point where it's pointless continuing," Dr Deaner says. Dr Tobin can't disagree.

My odds of now coming back are not even one per cent. I'm circling the drain. There's nothing left.

Or maybe not...

All of a sudden my heart rhythm changes and the wild electrical activity that has put me in this mess in the first place begins to settle down, to become more organised. My actual heart output is pathetically small but my heart is showing signs that it wants to behave. A glimmer of hope has appeared. For the first time in over an hour my heart begins doing what it is asked to do.

"Give me a pacing wire," Dr Deaner says, going back through the catheter in my groin, inching a temporary pacemaker all the way up to my heart, setting it in place at 90 beats a minute to help produce better electrical activity.

My heart responds by slowly, finally, starting to push some blood around my body. HOPE. HOPE. HOPE.

78 minutes after dying I'm back.

I'M BACK. I'm really, actually back.

#12

No-Man's Land

THE atmosphere in the cath lab shifts. Nobody can really believe that my heart has decided to click back into place.

"Let's try calcium chloride," Dr Deaner says, hoping that one final dose of hardcore drugs might help strengthen my heartbeat. My heart responds instantly, wondering what all the fuss has been about. Dr Deaner looks around at his colleagues, at all the people who have saved me, smiles and takes a moment for himself. He can't remember the last time a patient has been gone for so long before coming back. The room is euphoric but that only lasts a split-second as the focus shifts from my heart to the rest of me.

There's still no way I'm gonna pull through. There's still no way I can walk out of the London Chest Hospital.

If I make it through the night then I'm doing well. I'm still as good as dead. My brain hasn't functioned for almost 90 minutes. Almost a full football match. My heart might be beating again but what's the point if my brain has been starved of oxygen for so long?

Dr Deaner approaches the gaffer and dad, who has just arrived along with my brother, Daniel, and Mr Gartside.

"The good news is that we have got his heart working eventually but it is very early days," he says. "He may not wake up and even if he does then there is a risk he will be brain damaged. We have to wait and see."

After a cardiac arrest, patients are put in cold storage for at least 24 hours and I'm no different. Your body is basically shut down to give your organs a chance to take a breather and prepare for the fight ahead. The team looking after me have cooled down many, many people in their careers. Peter's hunch that a cath lab is the best place for me looks better by the minute.

At 8pm it's time for me to move into intensive care even if my chances are laughably small. This isn't a five-minute job and I'm connected to a mobile ventilator for the trip to the first floor.

Dr Deaner searches around for a pen as he realises he's not taken a single note so far this evening. Why would he? He should be unchaining his bike about now, not wiping my blood off his theatre blues.

He begins to note down what's happened while discussing with Dr Mohiddin whether a balloon pump, which helps improve the flow of the blood through the arteries, will be needed. They try and get as much advice as they can from everyone in the cath lab but both agree that at the moment any heavy-duty surgery is a waste of time. My heart is actually doing ok. How long that will last nobody knows. In intensive care, heavy sedative drugs enter my bloodstream through a drip while a cooling blanket is laid on me to make my body temperature plummet. The doctors call it 'therapeutic hypothermia'.

At the same time, Shauna and Suki jump into a silver Mercedes at Euston and begin the journey to the London Chest Hospital. It's raining and gloomy as Shauna sits in the back repeating the same line over and over again. "I hope he's alive," she is telling Suki. "I just hope he's alive."

Warwick has beaten Shauna to London by about 45 minutes after a journey full of bad phone reception, confusion as to where I'm heading, plus several calls from journalists, all trying to find out what is happening.

He is in complete professional mode and is refusing to let the situation get to him. What do I need? What does Shauna need? What does dad need? How do we manage the media? Which hotel are we all going to stay in tonight?

When he arrived at Euston he had 35 missed calls. This is a man in demand. He's already walked into the hospital and seen the gaffer, who is in total shock, in reception. He's already spoken to Dr Tobin who doesn't wrap it up.

"I might as well tell you this straight," Dr Tobin says.

"I don't think he's going to survive and if he does his chances of not being brain damaged are this," he adds, holding his fingers an inch apart to show Warwick that I'm in serious trouble.

Dr Mohiddin has the same opinion as Dr Tobin. And when he speaks to dad he has to tell him what he thinks, as sympathetically as he can. Dr Mohiddin doesn't know how much medical experience dad has or whether he watches every hospital drama on telly and believes that someone can always be saved.

At this moment in time it looks like my chances are tiny.

Dr Mohiddin has the perfect opportunity to build up a relationship with dad because they are next-door neighbours. Dr Mohiddin was born in Kampala in Uganda, not too far from where dad was born in Congo. So the two of them stand there, in a hospital in Bethnal Green, discussing my condition in Swahili. Can this night get any stranger?

"Is he still alive?" are Shauna's first words when she sees Warwick, who gives her a hug. He's organised for her car to sneak in through the back entrance to avoid the ever growing number of reporters who are gathering at the front of the hospital.

"Yes, he's still alive," says Warwick. Shauna is the coolest person in London right about now. She knows she needs to be positive, strong and there for me. Crying won't solve anything at the moment.

She walks up to intensive care and says hi to some visitors who have started turning up. Comedian Eddie Kadi is a good mate of mine and is here, as is my team-mate Tyrone Mears. The gaffer, and our press guy, Mark Alderton, are also in there. Tyrone had been injured for today's game and was still in the north-west when I collapsed.

The first thing he did was jump in his car and head to London.

Owen sends Kevin home but the gaffer wants him to be available on his mobile at all times. Owen knows that the guys want rapid updates and it's better if Kevin goes back with them so Owen can contact him with any important information, which he can then spread around. There's no point both of them knowing what's happening but the rest of the team being clueless.

Shauna comes into intensive care to see me along with Warwick. She needs all her strength but it's all too much. I'm freezing cold and I look dead. Tubes are hanging out of every part of me.

Shauna bursts into tears, places her head on Warwick's shoulder and shouts "it's not Fab, it's not Fab, it doesn't look like Fab". She grabs my hand and squeezes tightly, feeling my rapidly cooling palms. "I'm here now, I'm here now, Fab, you're gonna be ok."

She sits next to me and speaks to the intensive care nurse hovering at the end of my bed. "He doesn't deserve this," she tells her. "He's a good man, a good father, he gives money to the church, he's a good human being. Why has this happened to my Fab? If anything it should be me in that bed – he's way nicer than me."

She would give everything she owns, everything in the bank, everything that football has given her back in an instant, just to have me sit up and smile.

After the initial shock she flicks a switch and enters whirlwind mode. She kisses me on the lips, shoots back into the waiting room and picks up a Bible from family friend Mariama who has turned up. She comes back in, holds my hand again and she starts reading psalms to me for an hour. I read the Bible every day. She knows this is comforting me, even if I'm too cold, too ill to say it. Shauna feels far better after reading to me and her confidence rises. She comes out and tells everybody to go home, there's nothing they can do tonight, their prayers are very helpful but she understands if people want to leave.

Dad is downstairs talking to someone important.

He's in the hospital's prayer room asking God for help. Shauna walks in and Uncle Paul is also in there along with a few of dad's Congolese mates. He sees Shauna and his faith is rock solid. "They gave me a leaflet about how to cope with somebody affected by a cardiac arrest," he tells Shauna. "I've thrown it in the bin. He's going to be absolutely fine. I know that he's going to be absolutely fine."

Meanwhile, Owen has gone on a shopping spree.

"That'll be £104 please mate," the newsagent says.

"No problem," Owen replies.

The gaffer is stood in the only shop he can find open after midnight, buying six toothbrushes, six deodorants, six toothpastes, crisps, chocolate and a ton of other stuff for himself and the rest of the Bolton crew who have just left the hospital with him – Dr Tobin, Andy Mitchell, Mark Alderton, Tyrone and club journalist Rob Urbani.

The only clothes they've got are the ones they're stood up in.

The newsagent looks at the gaffer with a curious smile on his face. He sees the 'OC' initials on his jumper and works the rest out himself.

"So, you're from Bolton then?" he asks. "Good luck with everything, our prayers are with you."

They all get back to the hotel and Owen stands in the lobby handing out toothbrush after toothbrush, Coke can after Coke can, trying to work out how today has come to this.

"See you in the morning," Shauna says and kisses me again. She leaves at 4am with Suki and dad and they head for the Malmaison hotel in Farringdon. Warwick left an hour ago to try and get some sleep. He knows he faces one of the most important days of his life in a few hours time.

Don't we all.

Shauna and Suki collapse in bed as I lie frozen stiff overnight. I'm in no-man's land at the moment. Not dying, not living. Not getting better, not getting worse.

At breakfast, Shauna gets eggs on toast and fruit salad but pushes them both away. There's no way she can eat. Dad repeats what he said yesterday. He is a quiet man but gets his point across easily. "I know he's going to be ok. I believe that God will not let us down. We will all be fine."

As Owen travels to the hospital his phone beeps to let him know he's got a text message. He doesn't recognise the number.

'Hi Owen, it's David Beckham here,' it reads.

'I'm devastated by the news. I just want to know how Fabrice is. We're all thinking of him. If you get a moment and could let me know what's happening I'd be grateful. Thanks, David.'

David has tracked down Owen's number from somebody and wanted to pass on his best, wanted to join the millions of others hoping I can survive.

Everyone arrives at the hospital, all desperate for news but there isn't much to report. The fact I'm still alive is more than anyone can hope for at this moment in time. The corridor and small waiting room outside intensive care are slowly filling up with family and friends desperate for information.

The good news is that there isn't any bad news.

Owen gives Shauna a cuddle and does his best to find the words to comfort her. She comes back in to say hello to me and she's more prepared this time. She knows what to expect, what I'm going to look like, how cold I feel, how dead I appear to be. She walks outside and sees my step-mum Gertrude for the first time but again it all gets a bit much. She bursts into tears on Gertrude's shoulder before Suki takes hold of her and does her best to make it all better.

But how can she make it better? Nobody knows what is going to happen when I'm warmed back up. Nobody can say whether

I will pull through or not. And even if I do what then? There are too many questions, too many hard times ahead.

Dr Mohiddin speaks to Shauna and dad and is impressed with how they are handling the situation. They are emotional but in control, they are upset but strong. Dr Mohiddin has spoken to family members in the past who have collapsed in front of him. There'll be none of that here.

Today is starting to drag for everyone apart from Warwick, Mark Alderton and Mark Mann, the hospital's communication boss. The three of them stand in a side room trying to work out their response to what has become the biggest story in the country. All three want to keep speculation to a minimum so they discuss how to give the media accurate updates on my condition without turning the situation into a circus. One minute I could be up, the next I could be down. One minute I could be alive, the next I could be dead. If they're speaking to the media every five minutes then that won't help anyone.

Owen is drafted in to front up the press conferences and is briefed to say as much as possible while saying as little as possible at the same time. He walks outside, still in his Bolton tracksuit, and gets hit from all angles. But he's spoken to the media many times and handles it all well. No false hope is given but no gloomy predictions either. After today he will do all media interviews in the suit he gets sent down from home but for now his tracksuit will have to do.

As the day progresses all anyone can do is watch the clock. I've quite literally been put on ice. There's nothing to do but sit around, pray, drink NHS tea and wait until the experts in intensive care decide it's time to warm me back up to see what's underneath.

Mr Gartside has made his way back to the hospital after returning to the north-west late last night. He headed back down in convoy with Phil Mason this morning. Phil was a Methodist minister for 19 years before becoming our official club chaplain 12 months ago. Mr Gartside rang Phil at home last night and suggested he get down to London. Bolton want to offer all the help they can to Shauna and dad and they believe Phil can help. They aren't lying.

I pray with Phil before every game and whenever else I need strength. Now seems like as good a time as any.

Phil approaches Shauna and asks if he can see me. "Of course," Shauna says and she walks Phil through into intensive care. He holds my right hand with his left, juggling a Bible in the other, and he begins to read Psalm 121. He knows it's one of my favourites, he knows I need to hear the message it provides.

> *'I will lift up mine eyes unto the hills, from whence cometh my help. My help cometh from the Lord, which made heaven and earth'.*

I look lifeless and grim. 'Where is this going to end?' thinks Phil. 'Where do we go from here?'

Shauna is so strong and her spirit rubs off on everyone and everything. "Pray for him, Phil," she says. "Pray that he will be ok."

Phil holds my cold hand again and prays for strength, peace and healing and he gets emotional.

Although Phil is upset, the atmosphere is anything but depressing and because I'm still alive, the morale of everyone in the hospital is slowly starting to creep up.

"Can you keep the noise down please, this is a hospital," the nurse hisses down the corridor outside intensive care as grown adults try to bite their tongues to stop laughing.

You'd never know my life is in the balance 15 metres through the double doors. Eddie Kadi is back in the hospital and he's ensuring the atmosphere has become crazy positive, doing his best to keep everyone's spirits up. Shauna and Phil walk back into the waiting room and Shauna has a big grin on her face as she hears the chat and the gossip. She is being so positive and that is rubbing off on Eddie and Owen, on everyone.

Eddie might be a professional comedian but, for once, he's met his match in the gaffer. Eddie tells a story, the gaffer tells a story, Eddie tells a story, the gaffer tells a story. On and on it goes.

"In training I split the guys into three teams and nominate three captains," Owen begins. "Of course only two teams can play at any one time so I then ask a stupid question and the first captain to answer gets to play first before picking which other team to play against."

Everyone in the corridor turns to listen. Eddie is thinking of his next comeback, Mr Gartside, Phil, Dr Tobin, Shauna and Mark Alderton all settle in for the gaffer's latest tale. He's done some after-dinner speaking in the past so he cruises into gear, giving Eddie a real workout. A guy from Congo is sparring with a man from Paisley in a hospital corridor in London. Suki is also throwing her stories and chatter into the mix. Somehow it all works. Three very different people have clicked and the atmosphere is buzzing.

"So anyways," Owen continues. "This one day I split the guys up and I pick three blokes who I think will give me a stupid answer. I pick David Wheater, Mark Davies and Chris Eagles. I then ask them the oldest question in the book. 'What do you put in a toaster?' and as quick as a flash David Wheater goes 'toast'. That's not even the funny bit. Mark Davies, who is laughing the loudest, then turns around and deadly serious goes 'no, crumpets.'"

It's daft, it's stupid, it's exactly what everyone needs. Laughing beats crying.

"Jason Scotland knocked on my door one day at St Johnstone," Owen carries on.

"'Gaffer, I need some new boots,'" he said.

"Tell me what size you are Jase and I will get it sorted."

"'Well, boss, sometimes I'm an eight, sometimes I'm a nine.'

"Well what shoe size do you take?'"

"Jeez boss, am I getting a pair of shoes as well?'"

The afternoon becomes the evening and people have again started to drift away. Experts from all over the hospital are monitoring my heart rate, my ventilation and have begun to discuss my kidney function, with urine, blood and imaging tests. They're not working. That doesn't fill anyone with confidence.

Shauna pops in before she heads back to the hotel, kisses me and asks me to do all I can to pull through.

"Be strong," she says. "You're a fighter Fab, you need to fight harder than ever."

The next time she sees me I could be dead, or as good as dead, or severely brain damaged. I could be God knows what.

Tomorrow (Monday) is crunch time. She gets back to the hotel, gets in the shower and begins to sob to herself about the situation, about how much she misses her Fab and Joshua, about how unfair it all is. The uncertainty of the future has sent her spinning and as she falls asleep she knows she's about to be tested like never before.

"I've got a great feeling," she says in the morning, turning to her right to see Suki lying next to her in their double bed. "I just have a feeling that it's going to be ok. I can't explain it."

She repeats the phrase to Warwick at breakfast, again pushing away her food before he does his best to back her up. "Well," he says. "A women's intuition is never wrong. Let's go and show everyone that he's going to come back."

As Shauna, Warwick and everyone from Bolton return to the hospital the decision has already been made to bring me out of my induced coma.

At 6am the drugs were removed and the cooling blankets taken off. If I'm to survive my brain has to start working and working soon.

I've been moved into my own room – nicknamed 'The Beckham Room' because David's dad once stayed in there – and yesterday's jolly atmosphere has been replaced with fear and concern once again. If I'm going to pull through, the next few hours will be critical.

Dr Mohiddin has now become the consultant in charge of my care, picking up from Dr Deaner because he specialises in heart muscle diseases, which appears to be what caused all this trouble in the first place. But he is only one of many experts now trying to bring me back.

He is the captain of the best team I've ever seen play.

Dr Mohiddin can see what I mean to Shauna and dad and Gertrude and Owen and Dr Tobin and Warwick and Suki and Eddie and everyone else. He doesn't want to have to deliver bad news to all these people, these new people who he has come to admire in such a small amount of time.

He is also a doctor who has never been in the spotlight before. The national and international media interest adds another layer of pressure. On Saturday night and last night he travelled home, turned on the TV and saw his patient as the main story. It all feels very odd. As the morning starts to get older, Shauna comes in and sits next to me. 'Whatever happens over the next few hours happens,' she says to herself. 'I'm not leaving him. If we can't have any more kids or if he needs a carer or whatever, I'm going nowhere.' What a woman. Dr Mohiddin has a quiet word with Shauna and dad and tries to prepare them for every possibility, to try and emotionally get them ready for whatever will happen today.

And before anyone knows it I start to stir.

Waking up from a coma takes time. Your brain is rebooting itself slowly. Dr Mohiddin cannot believe I've started to come around so quickly, in fact he didn't expect me to wake up today, if at all.

But there's no switch that can be instantly flicked, no lights immediately come on, I don't get up and start dancing.

And just because I'm now awake doesn't mean I'm out of the woods yet. Shauna comes in again and my eyes are rolling around in my head.

This is a bad sign. This is a bad sign.

'Well that's it now then,' she thinks, as calm as anything but at the same time terrified. 'He's brain damaged.'

That thought barely lasts a second though as the doctor who accompanies her into intensive care sets to work.

"Fabrice," the doctor whispers.

And I move my head to my right, searching for the face that just mentioned my name.

I've responded.

I'm alive. I'm not brain damaged. I'M A MIRACLE.

#13

Second Life

WAKING up in hospital was the strangest day of my life. I felt like my head was a pillow – big and soft and cloudy. What am I doing in a hospital? It felt like a dream, as if I'd fallen into a deep sleep and then didn't know where I was when I woke up.

It was like the weirdest sleepwalk. Except, of course, I wasn't walking. You try walking when you're hooked up to every hospital machine in England. I couldn't move. My body was telling me that moving at that moment was a very, very bad idea. Where am I?

As I opened my eyes I've never, EVER felt worse. Think of the worst hangover you've ever had then add a whole new level on top. Groggy, exhausted, useless.

It felt like I was dying. I looked down and saw this hospital gown covering me up. Two big pillows and a hospital gown? Is this a wind up? I couldn't even begin to understand this situation.

What is going on here?

I looked around to my left and right, trying to absorb the noises, and work out where I was. Where am I? Just total confusion. I had a head full of fluff but I looked again to my right to see Shauna.

Eh? What is Shauna doing here? What am I doing here? Where is 'here' anyhow?

Question, questions, questions.

"Where is Josh?" were my first whispered words. "Where am I? What happened? Is Josh ok?"

My skin felt like it wasn't part of my body. At that moment in time, somebody had stolen my arms and legs and my brain felt brainless. I'd had better days.

I then moved my right hand up to my nose to remove my oxygen mask and croaked out "what's going on?" Shauna, being the boss, soon put me straight. "Put the mask back on and I will tell you what happened," she said.

I did what she asked and she told me I had collapsed playing football at White Hart Lane and that I hadn't been breathing for 78 minutes before coming back.

Ha ha, whatever. For real?

Me? I don't collapse. There ain't nobody in the Premier League as fit as Fabrice Muamba.

I pulled the mask back down and slowly repeated what Shauna

had said. "Me? Collapsed?" I thought there was a joke going on. "Really?" and she answered "yeah, really."

And then – bang – I passed out again. I suppose I thought I better try and get back to sleep so I could wake up from this dream. You don't come round straight away from something like this. Your body warms back up in stages and I was constantly drifting off, sometimes being ok and other times waking up clueless.

Later on in the first day of my second life, two strangers came into my room and stood next to my bed. Dr Mohiddin, a bloke I would come to know as Dr Sam, and his colleague Dr Deaner tried to explain to me what had happened.

Who is this guy? Who is speaking to me? When does the second half start? I'm still convinced this is a joke and that none of this is actually happening.

Dr Deaner stood close to me and said: "I've heard you're a good footballer," and I said: "I try to be, I'm ok."

He then whispered what had happened and what treatment I had received. I wasn't listening. I was wondering who was behind this stitch-up.

Dr Deaner had tears in his eyes and Dr Sam was the same. Whoever these men were, they really seemed to be caring for me, which was nice.

Where am I again? In hospital? For real?

After Dr Deaner left, Dad came in into the room and did his best to put me at ease.

I cannot tell you how scary it is when you're in a dream that won't end. I wanted to know where, who, why, when – I wanted some answers and some answers fast.

"Are you ok?" dad asked. "How are you feeling?"

I told him I was ok and that I was just confused.

"Don't worry, it will all become clear," he said. "Just concentrate on getting better. God has saved you from this mess and when you start recovering I will explain everything."

Next thing I know dad left and Aunt Fifi walked in. I went through the same process again, asking what was going on, but she repeated, almost word for word, what dad had said.

"Relax, recover, we will tell you all about it later on. You are a miracle boy – this is unbelievable."

That wasn't good enough and I wanted some answers quicker than that. If I was a miracle then tell me why. Stop telling me later, later, later. I wanted to know what was happening. Tell me now.

The early stages followed the same pattern.

"Shauna, Shauna, what happened?"

"You collapsed and had a cardiac arrest," she would answer.

"For real?"

"Yes, for real."

That scene was played out every two minutes.

I had so many drugs in me I could barely stay awake for an hour. I would hang on for as long as I could before slipping away. Oh my God, I was so weak. As weak as a baby.

Shauna was amazing throughout all of this. She kept coming back in and telling me it was all going to be ok. She knew something I didn't.

Where am I again? In hospital? For real?

As well as being confused I was hooked up to every sort of drip, kidney machine, heart monitor – you name it. It looked like somebody had died in there.

The gaffer came in at one point to see how I was doing. I noticed that the tie he was wearing wasn't the official club tie that is used on matchdays. It was a slightly different style.

I've only just woken up from 78 minutes of nothing plus a medical coma and I'm able to spot the difference in the gaffer's tie from the other side of the room. He had tears in his eyes too. He just couldn't work out why I looked ok.

Where am I again? In hospital? For real?

Others drifted in and out while I drifted in and out. Shauna brought Phil Mason in at some point on the first day and I immediately knew who he was. "Fab, the club chaplain is here," she said.

"Phil!' was my response as I turned my head on the pillow. "How are you?" He was close to tears too. Why is everyone crying?

Where am I again? In hospital? For real?

The last person I can remember coming into my room on that first day was Warwick.

"Are you ok mate?" he said.

"Yeah, I am – but what is going on?"

Me and Warwick are so close, he's like my second father. He is my agent first of all but he is a good man who knows me inside out and I owe him and all the guys at Key Sports Management so much. I found out later how much he and his team had done for me. If I'd known then I would've tried to get up and hug him.

I was so high on drugs that I could barely register who came in to see me and when. Johan Djorou was one of those and we spoke for a bit. "What's happening?" he said. "Nothing much," I replied. It was just like two mates chatting. I asked him for answers too but he didn't know anything either.

I didn't know at the time but in the corridor outside the intensive care unit there were doctors, nurses and all my family and friends amazed that I was alive and responding to their questions.

You've got to remember that if you fall off a ladder or you are in a bus crash or whatever, when you wake up you can probably remember a little bit of the build up to what happened. You can slowly piece together the past so you can work out why you're in a hospital bed. But I had none of that luck. I'd gone from kicking a football around to being surrounded by people crying just because when they asked me how I was I told them I was "ok."

It doesn't get much weirder than that and it really freaked me out.

Where am I again? In hospital? For real?

By the end of the first day my heart had already begun to show signs that it was completely back to normal. My heartbeat was strong and secure and the doctors were not really too concerned about it any longer. Of course, that didn't stop them doing an amazing job looking after me, I just mean that I had bigger problems elsewhere. Like my kidneys.

A total of 15 shocks before I arrived at hospital, plus the same number again in the cath lab, came at a cost and that cost was muscle. Tons of it.

During a cardiac arrest a huge amount of muscle can be damaged very quickly and those muscle fibres break down into the bloodstream. Dr Sam told me one day that the official name for it is 'rhabdomyolysis.' I think I'll stick with 'damaged muscle'.

Normally, your kidneys would be able to cope with all this extra hard work because that is what they do best; they clean out all the bad stuff in your blood.

But my kidneys had stopped working, just like the rest of me, and their filters were clogged up with all this new wasted muscle fibre. That meant I couldn't pee and I was placed on dialysis, through a big tube in my neck, which took the pressure off my kidneys and gave them a chance to heal themselves.

When you're out for the count as long as I was, your body basically closes down. Why wouldn't it? It thinks you're dead. After your brain, your kidneys suffer the most when they have no oxygen. I didn't have a clue about any of this at the time. I was to spend a month learning the hard way that your kidneys can cause you real troubles.

Dr Sam came in and stood over my bed and said "we will do all we can to make you better, the only thing holding you back is your kidneys." He told me it was early stages yet but he gave me the confidence that I would get back on my feet.

Where am I again? In hospital? For real?

My memory problems continued during that first week and I started getting on my own nerves, never mind anyone else's. My brain was wiped clean every time I went to sleep, every time I was put to bed for the night. Shauna would leave the room for two minutes and when she came back in I would be back to where we started. Her patience was brilliant until she finally decided to sort it out once and for all.

FABRICE MUAMBA, MARCH 23, LONDON CHEST HOSPITAL, COLLAPSED PLAYING FOOTBALL

The words, written in felt tip, were big and bold on a whiteboard at the end of my bed. Shauna and my doctors had decided I could answer my own questions.

There were photos of me with Shauna, plus snaps of Joshua on the whiteboard, which all made me realise and remember what I had and who I was.

During those first days, playing football again was not on anyone's mind. I had nothing on my mind at all actually – I was still totally out of it. My main concern was just to get better, even if I was still frustrated with the lack of straight answers.

Nobody could tell me what had happened because nobody knew why I'd collapsed.

It remains that way to this day. All the expertise and science and whatever in the world and my cardiac arrest is as big a mystery now as it was when I hit the pitch at White Hart Lane.

Dr Sam tried his best to explain my situation and he gave me the faith to believe I would improve.

He put things into my language and would speak to me on my own. I was just incredibly frustrated and angry with everything. How dare this happen to me?

What had I done to deserve this?

As I slowly improved and could stay awake for longer, I knew it was time to try and get out of bed.

To begin to get my life back.

#14

Starting Over

I REMEMBER trying to move properly for the first time and it seemed like the most important thing I'd ever done. Me and Shauna were in the room and she said she would be there to help teach me how to walk again.

I wanted to get out of bed after less than a week but I had to wait to be given permission. Eventually Dr Sam told me I could try.

I wished I'd never asked.

Shauna sat next to me and she tried to give me all the encouragement I would need. "Just swing your legs around to the right, I will catch you," she said.

It was as simple as that. Five minutes ago I was a midfielder in the Premier League, one of the fittest guys in the country, and now my only goal is to try and swing out of bed and stand up.

Even though Shauna was right next to me supporting me I was scared about trying to get up which didn't help. Not only was my body hurting but my brain was as well. What if it happened again? What if my heart failed me for the second time? It was a terrifying moment that played on my mind.

I don't want to die, not here, not again.

It was so hard. My whole body was screaming in pain and aches. I can remember my muscles were shaking and I was sweating.

I was starting again. I was like a baby.

"Try and move your leg," Shauna said.

"I'm trying, I'm trying," I snapped back in frustration. But she took it slowly and she helped me brilliantly, encouraging me by holding my hand and trying to make the atmosphere nice and relaxed.

I finally managed to swing around and hauled myself onto my feet. I can remember now how cold the hospital floor was, how weird it felt to be standing, how dizzy I felt, how much I needed Shauna's help and support.

I stood for about a minute and then collapsed back on the bed, completely exhausted. I stood up five times that day. That was it. Stand up, wait 60 seconds, lie down. To look at me you would've thought I'd run a marathon.

Although physically I was exhausted I was also really pleased. That was the start of my comeback and they may only have been tiny, tiny steps, but you've got to start somewhere. I had to piece all these bits together and begin again. It was about getting my confidence back and proving to myself that I was alive and well.

Somehow, I was alive and well – apart from my kidneys.

I was trying to eat and drink normally but the wastes from what I was drinking weren't going anywhere. My face, hands and toes became so swollen because I couldn't get rid of all the fluid my body was creating. I became so fat! All this stuff was building up and I was worried about what I looked like. I didn't want to scare the ton of visitors I had, especially during that first week, even if I wasn't allowed to see most of them.

Ashley Cole, Shaun Wright-Phillips, Gary Cahill, Emmanuel Adebayor and Michael Essien all came to the hospital but never got up the stairs to intensive care. There were just too many people, too much stress and noise for the staff there, too much publicity going on at the time. Most players who turned up were greeted in a side room by dad or Warwick and thanked for turning up. It was truly appreciated then and now. But, practically speaking, the hospital couldn't cope with so many wanting to say 'hi' so the side room downstairs became like a second waiting room. Cousins and friends from school would show up and whoever was free would go down and explain the situation, then people would leave.

Thierry Henry visited on the Tuesday of the first week – the only problem is I was so out of it I had no idea he had even been.

Eh? Thierry? Whatever. Shut up. He lives in America.

It took some convincing to be told that he had raced across the Atlantic to see me. I couldn't remember a thing. We were chatting the day before it happened and then dad came in and said "Thierry has been here."

"Has he?" I said. He'd heard about what had happened and

immediately flown all the way from New York and I couldn't even remember it. This legend of the game, the guy who once took the piss out of me as a young teenager, flew all the way from America just to show he cared. Nobody knew he had been to see me. He snuck in through the back door of the hospital, met Shauna and dad and everyone else, then snuck away again just as quickly.

That shows you what kind of guy he is, what kind of man he is. He flew straight back to America after the visit and wore an arm-band with my name on it when the New York Red Bulls played the Colorado Rapids in their next game. He scored twice so I obviously brought him some luck! When I went back to New York in June he gave me that armband and we had a laugh and a joke about everything. I admire him so much – too much!

James Vaughan was a regular visitor and some of the Bolton guys also came in during that first week and they really lifted my spirits. The goalkeeper Rob Lainton came in to see me. He is a good bloke who I've grown close to. He was so relieved to find me looking ok and we both got emotional about the situation.

Zat Knight and Nigel Reo-Coker also said 'hi'. The last time they'd seen me I'd been having my chest pumped in public. Their visit remains a hazy memory but I remember Nigel telling me how pleased all the guys were that I was fighting hard.

"I'm glad you're back," he said. "You're back with us. You worried us for a bit."

Liam Brady from Arsenal came in to keep his eye on me, the same as he had always done. "How are you doing?" he asked. I told him I was fine and thanked him for his support. He told me to ring him if I needed anything. You don't realise how many people you know or how generous they can be until something like this happens.

Robert Pires arrived one day and he leant down and gave me a big hug as I sat in my chair. "You're looking better than last time I saw you," he joked. It was just great to talk about football and what was going on. General chat. I respect him so much because he was a senior player when I was just a kid at Arsenal so his visit meant a lot.

Johan was there all the time, Justin was the same, as was Rashid. They are my boys, my friends from years back. They've known me from a very young age and they know me better than anyone. One of the most touching guests was Ivan Klasnic, one of my best mates in the game. Ivan has had his own kidney problems and has had a double transplant. If anyone knew the fear I was feeling, the uncertainty, the frustration, then it was him.

"Everyone loves you," he said. "Why you, nobody deserves this."

"I know, but that's life," I replied. If this was God's plan then I just had to get on with it and cope. We spoke and he hugged me. "We are all here for you," he said.

The visitors just kept on coming and it was great to see so many different people so concerned about me.

Mark Halsey, the Premier League referee, arrived to represent the Referees' Association, Bobby Barnes from the PFA, David Bernstein from the FA and Dave Richards from the Premier League all showed up. I've never been as popular in my life! I didn't think so many important people cared so much and it was great for them to take the time out, even if I was in what felt like a constant daze. I slept so much it was ridiculous. Sleep, sleep, sleep was all I did. Most people tried to protect me from the truth and the seriousness of what had happened to me and at that point that was fine with me. I needed rest more than anything.

As I slept, Shauna and Warwick were being hit from all angles by the media who wanted the first picture of me in hospital but they were determined to put my recovery first. There were some worries that a picture of me would be leaked out so every visitor was warned about taking any snaps of me in case they ended up in the wrong hands. In the end Shauna solved it by putting her own picture of me on Twitter to show people I was doing ok. She wanted everybody to see I was fighting hard, not just the readers of one newspaper or another. It was typical Shauna, the best problem-solver I know.

#####

Shauna rented an apartment near the hotel so she brought me food every day and I also saw Dad and Gertrude all the time as well. I'm not really a 'huggy' person so there weren't that many really emotional moments but it was wonderful to see them and to know I had such back up.

However, the best moment of the lot was seeing Joshua. I didn't see him for so long when I was inside because we didn't want him around the whole situation. It could've been scary for the little man and I didn't want him to be upset.

When I first saw him I was sat in the chair next to my bed, dressed in my cool hospital gown as always, and he ran through the door shouting "daddy, daddy." It did my morale so good to see him. I was still very weak and Joshua climbed all over me from the start.

At this point I still had probes and fluid lines sticking out of everywhere. He jumped on my lap and said "daddy, everyone at school is talking about you."

Then he said: "Let me take this out" before trying to disconnect all those wires attached to my chest and neck!

"Whoa, whoa," I said. "Calm down, daddy isn't well!"

It was so funny and great to see him. He was there for about 35 minutes and it did me the world of good. I had my family back. The craziest thing was I could tell the difference in his development in the short amount of time I'd been away.

All parents know that you only have to turn away for a second and your kids have grown up and Joshua was no different. Laughter is the best medicine and I felt great when he left because he always makes me smile. I gave him a big kiss as he went out of the door because he's a special boy in many ways and that undoubtedly helped.

I was starting to get tiny glimpses of the outside world and what the reaction to my situation had been. I was shocked when I found out that Bolton's game against Aston Villa had been postponed. We were meant to be travelling to Villa Park on the Tuesday after the FA Cup match on the Saturday but some idiot collapsed and that was the end of that.

It was Shauna who broke the news to me days later.

"Bolton's game was called off," she said while sitting next to my bed. "Why?" I said.

"Because of you," she said. "You're not the same Fabrice anymore. The world is changing out there. When you come out you will see what I mean."

I had heard that there'd been a big response to my situation but I was so close to events that I had no idea how the world was reacting. There were no mobiles allowed in my room and I didn't see a television or read a newspaper. I was clueless at the time to the scale of the prayers and the attention I was receiving.

For example, on the Tuesday after I collapsed, Phil Mason put on a service at the Reebok Stadium in the chairman's suite thinking that maybe 30 people would show up.

He had to put more chairs out in the end.

Sixty members of staff came to pray and to speak to Phil about me and my situation. He also opened up the suite to members of the public and he got a ton of cards and emails from people all over the world praying for me and asking how I was.

Without knowing it, I was going from being me to being someone known by the whole country. When I did finally get out of hospital, that would prove to be very weird indeed.

One thing I have to repeat loud and proud is how much I owe Bolton following my collapse. The club has been amazing.

They did everything in their power to help me and I will always, always, always be grateful to the club for what they have done for me. They quite literally couldn't have done anything else to bring me back to full health.

As a patient the club were sensational. They have stuck by me through thick and thin and I have nothing but the utmost respect for everybody there. I'm so grateful for all their care and attention. They weren't the only ones. Later on, while still in hospital, I started to get loads of messages from well-wishers and I was so touched by that. It felt very strange to be the centre of all this attention but it was a reminder of how good the British public are.

In the end I would need all the support I could get. My recovery wouldn't be as straightforward as I hoped. There were some difficult moments ahead before I could really see the light at the end of a long, dark tunnel.

#15

Lost And Found

'WHERE is she? Where has she gone now?' I thought to myself. I was getting more agitated by the minute.

I waited. Still no sign of Shauna. I waited a few more seconds. Still nothing. My eyes focused on the door of the hospital room. I waited for it to open but still nothing.

What am I doing here? I've had enough. I want to get out. Why has this happened to me? Why me?

Just then, Shauna appeared again. I lost control.

"Why did you go for so long? Where have you been? Don't go anywhere," I shouted at her.

"Fab, I was looking after you," she replied, astonished. "I went to try and help you and get you better." My head wouldn't listen to her answers.

It was the second week of being in hospital and Shauna had gone outside to ask the doctor on duty about my medication. She must have been out of the room for two minutes, maybe three at the most. But I was so impatient and frustrated and angry that I just exploded.

I repaid the woman who had stood by me with abuse. I just couldn't help all this frustration pouring out. It wasn't the only time I let things get on top of me. Deep down, I felt so bad about how I was behaving but I couldn't help it – it's as simple as that.

Shauna never once questioned her love for me or her faith in us as a couple when I was looking half-dead, in fact when I WAS half-dead, and I repaid her by trying to throw her out of my hospital room.

I was a confused and angry mess.

The public think I'm all smiles and most of the time I am a happy person but underneath that grin was a man feeling robbed of his future and worried about what that future even held. It was gloomy.

I cannot pretend that I was anything like the ideal patient. I had some dark moments. Times when I kicked people out of my room. Moments when I just wanted to be left alone.

I'd gone from being a fit young man to someone who couldn't walk. Just think about that for a moment. Think about what it must be like to have your health stolen from you in the time it takes to fall over.

I can tolerate most things and I'm pretty laid back. But when my anger comes out then there's no stopping me. Every day seemed to be the same. I knew that Dr Sam and his team were doing a

FABRICE **MUAMBA**

brilliant job and I was in the best place but that didn't make it any
easier. What can I say? I acted like an arsehole at times.

A frustrated and angry arsehole.

I had blood check after blood check. I hate needles and doctors
pushing and probing me to see what was going on so that was
hard to handle and I took my frustration out on Shauna.

"Get out," I would sulk. "I don't want to be with anyone."

It's hard to explain just how helpless I felt. To go from flying
into tackles in the Premier League to lying in a tiny room as the
wall gets closer and closer every day.

Shauna would be relieved when I needed something from outside, just so she could get out and snatch some fresh air. To be
stuck there, with tubes coming out of everywhere, was the most
difficult thing for me.

Everyone treated me so well and I would never complain about
the staff. But that doesn't mean it was easy to wake up every
morning, praying that my kidneys would work, only to spend all
day with nothing happening.

Everybody around me had a different outlook but I wouldn't listen to them. Shauna, Dad and Dr Sam were just grateful I wasn't
dead. If all I had to worry about was not being able to go to the
toilet then I should be happy.

You've got to remember that this was my crisis time. Not the
78 minutes when I was gone. That was when everyone else was
panicking, working at a million miles an hour to save my life.

I never saw or experienced any of the terror they did, from the
moment my skull crashed into the White Hart Lane turf to my
ambulance journey and my heart finally starting to work properly
again. I missed all that. It never affected me. I was at the centre
of all this pain and worry and I was the one person who was

bothered the least by it.

Now was different. Coming to terms with what had happened was tough to handle and I switched between moments of distress and confusion before sleep came to relieve me.

Every day ran into the one before it and the one after it. Sitting in a small room waiting, waiting, waiting. And also having to take a ton of drugs to help. When your kidneys fail you can end up with too much potassium or too little in your blood and it's important to keep an eye on it, especially in heart patients because potassium helps keep everything working properly.

Well, I had too little so I had to take supplements and it was disgusting. I dreaded it every day. The taste was just awful. Not even cup of tea after cup of tea would shift it. I never drank tea before collapsing but NHS tea changed that – I can't get enough of it now!

So, at times I was a snappy, moaning patient and I've apologised since. And rightly so. I want to tell you I was as clean as a whistle but I want to be honest – I wasn't. Nowhere near in fact.

Dr Sam could see the state I was in and he would tell me that I had beaten all the odds to still be around and that I should be proud of myself for surviving. Not many people go through what I did and I needed to hear that. His support alongside all his fellow doctors gave me some confidence and I was also helped by people visiting all day every day. My faith in God was always there as well which meant I could pray when I was feeling really down.

Shauna, dad and Dr Sam eventually saw my frustrations as a positive sign. As far as they were concerned if I was still alive enough to be upset about how things were going, then I was also driven enough to get on with rebuilding my life.

I should've left hospital in a hearse. A three-week delay in leaving on my feet was nothing as far as they were concerned.

After what seemed like forever, my kidneys finally started to slowly improve which was the break I had been desperately waiting for. Let me tell you how good Dr Sam and the rest of the team looking after me were.

You won't believe this.

Magdi Yaqoob is a professor of kidney medicine and was looking into what was wrong with me.

As my kidney trouble continued he turned to the rest of the team looking after me, including Dr Sam, and said "this isn't a problem, he will get better, I think Fabrice will pee exactly a week today."

And he was spot on. I pee'd to a timetable!

That goes to show you the quality and experience of the people looking after me. Dr Sam played a huge part but so did people like Dr Chris Broomhead, Dr Alistair Chesser, Dr Simon Harrod, Dr Kate Wark, David Wilson and a million others.

They all helped to put me back together and I will never forget the moment when I finally got the urge to go to the toilet – when the finish line finally appeared.

One day dad brought in some friends, including my Uncle Paul, and they came into my room to pray.

"We are here to pray for your kidneys," they said. That was fine by me but there's praying and there's praying and I know how loud these people can be!

I said: "Listen, dad, please pray but we're in hospital, so please keep it low-key." And they started to pray.

And pray. And pray. And pray. And pray.

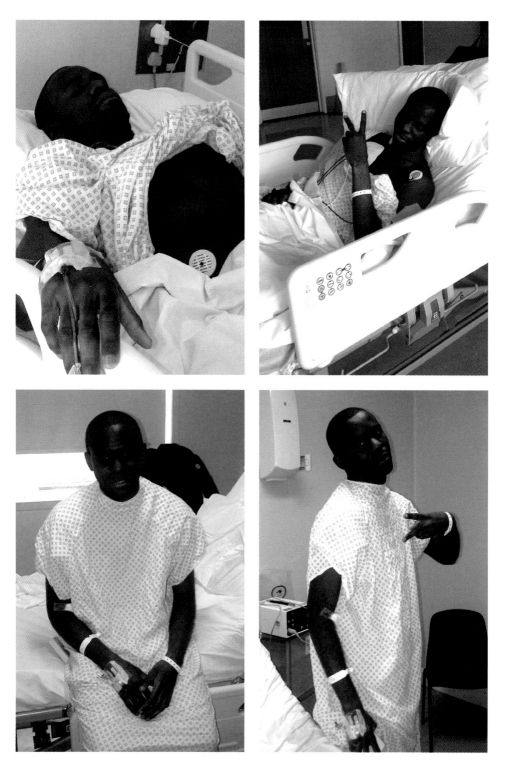

One step at a time: From White Hart Lane to the London Chest Hospital in the blink of an eye. The road to recovery wasn't easy and I couldn't have done it without the support of my family and friends, not to mention the amazing staff, who I'll always be in debt to

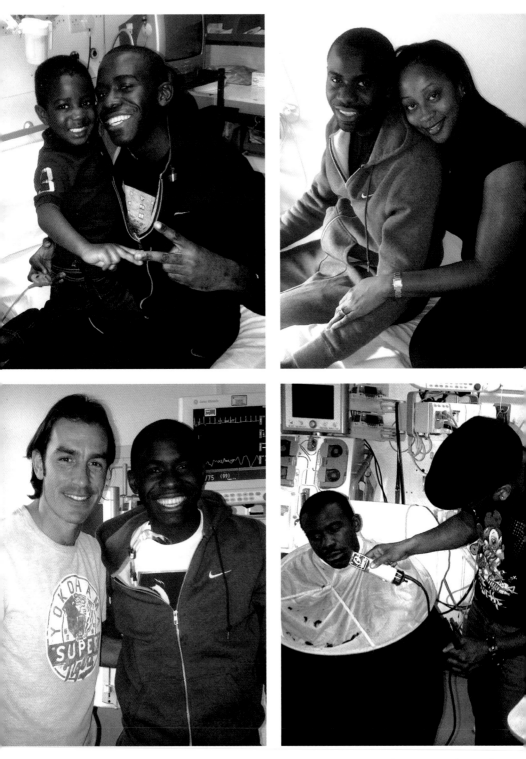

Smiling again: (Clockwise, from top) I was so happy to see Joshua, and Shauna was always there for me through the highs and lows. Getting back to normal life involved another shave and trim in hospital from Jhamal John, while Robert Pires was one of the many who came to visit

Message to the world: (Top) Owen Coyle, flanked by Bolton chairman Phil Gartside, talks to the press outside the hospital. (Above) The fans flocked to the Reebok Stadium in the days after my collapse. I was shocked when I realised how people had reacted

Uniting for Fabrice: Players from my clubs – Bolton (above, left), Birmingham (above, right) and Arsenal (below) showed their support for me by getting special t-shirts made

The football family: From Liverpool to Barcelona and beyond, I was touched by how the players and fans stood together in my hour of need. I never thought I'd see the day when Lionel Messi (above, centre) pulled on a Fabrice Muamba shirt!

Emotional day: I shed a tear or two when I returned to the Reebok – I wasn't the only one!

Heroes: (Left) The four brilliant doctors who saved my life. They are (from left): Dr Andrew Deaner, Dr Sam Mohiddin, Spurs' Dr Shabaaz Mughal and Bolton's Dr Jonathan Tobin. Right, top: Contemplating a return to football and (right, bottom) a shock appearance at the Bernabeu!

New life: (Top) Congratulating Chelsea on their FA Cup final win at Wembley and (above) picking up a degree from Bolton University. It was a real privilege to be asked to carry the Olympic Torch (left)

I'm back: (Below) Feeling a football at my feet again was special, even if it was just a holiday kickaround in Dubai

Homecoming: I couldn't believe the reception I got when I returned to Congo. (Top, right) Shauna and Joshua in the congregation and (right) with Pastor Claude

I'm a lucky man... looking forward to the future with my family

They surrounded my bed and Shauna was there as well. And they said "don't worry your kidneys will get better."

Pastor Nkosi, a well-known Congolese pastor based in Tottenham, also came to see me and spoke to me about faith.

He put his hands on my kidneys and told them to get moving. That everyone was bored with them not working. That it was time for them to sort themselves out. I had everyone fighting in my corner.

With all this help I had the confidence to believe I would get better. Medicine gets you so far and those involved with my treatment were beyond amazing, beyond incredible, beyond whatever words you want to use.

But sometimes you need some extra help...

As well as having all these people praying for me, I also spoke to mum in Congo. Can you imagine how worried she had been? I hadn't spoken to her since the incident so when I found a quiet moment in the room me and Shauna made the call.

"How are you, son?" she blurted out. She cried and cried and told me to listen to my doctors which I knew, deep down, I should do. As I lay there in the room, holding Shauna's hand and speaking to my mum, who had been petrified that her son was dead, I realised how important it was to pull through and to continue living a good life, an honest life, my life.

Mum told me that in Congo everybody at the local church has been praying for me. She wanted me to call the pastor of that church. So I did.

In the Congolese community you must understand that we think prayer can do anything. We believe it can move mountains, it can change the world, it can heal everything.

I spoke to the pastor who insisted we prayed over the phone.

Me in London, him in Kinshasa. "Come on God, make it happen," I said. So we prayed and prayed and when we said "Amen" I SWEAR that the urge to pee started. I filled bottle after bottle, grinning like an idiot – just because I could go to the toilet!

When my kidneys woke up it was another sign I was inching towards safety. My appetite came back with a bang, I wanted to get living again, get back to normality.

The only problem is that what used to be normal was no longer possible. I was looking at the end of my career, the one thing I had loved all my life.

During my time in intensive care, Professor Richard Schilling became involved in my treatment. He's far too modest to admit it but he's one of the best heart specialists in the world. His area of expertise is heart rhythm problems and he's taught all over the planet on the subject. He's basically the man.

And it was his job to tell me that I would need something called an Implantable Cardioverter Defibrillator (ICD). That is basically a device that sits on your heart and monitors its rhythm and if there is a problem with it and you go into cardiac arrest it delivers a shock to sort you out.

I was in two minds about whether I needed the ICD or not. On the one hand, getting the ICD put in meant I could leave hospital as soon as possible and try and get on with my life. It would be my leaving present from those who had looked after me. But on the other hand my faith is so strong that I didn't see the point of having it done. Dr Sam did his best to convince me, day after day, that it was the best thing for me and Shauna would also get stuck in and tell me to stop being stupid and get it done.

I must admit, though, that I didn't really want it. "Whatever, I'm not interested," was my thinking. My attitude was that my kidneys were working so let's get out of here. The last thing I wanted was more hospital time, even if they did try and explain that the ICD was just like a seatbelt in a car. You hope it will never have to be put to test but it's better to have it there than take the risk. But, really, what can it do? Is it really going to save my life if things go bad again? I'm not sure.

As always it was Shauna who finally made me agree to the operation even if she used some low tactics to make it happen!

She couldn't understand why I wanted to put myself back at risk and she threatened all sorts, including packing her bags and going, unless I woke up and had it put in.

The best thing she did was contact Khalilou Fadiga, the former Bolton player who also suffered a cardiac arrest on the pitch back in 2004. If anyone knew what I was going through then it was him.

Shauna got Suki to ring El-Hadji Diouf for Khalilou's number and she managed to get hold of him at home in Belgium and explained the situation.

"Fabrice needs an ICD but he's not keen," she said. "Will you come and speak to him please and explain its importance. I will sort the flights out and pay for everything."

"You're insulting me," Khalilou replied. "I will happily come over. But I'm paying for the flights."

The way he visited me shows everything you need to know about how good a man he is but I still didn't want the ICD. Khalilou spoke to me and told me it didn't take long and that I wouldn't feel a thing. He was straight and just told me how it was.

Shauna also chipped away at me for hours at a time. But I thought – and I still think now – that God wants me to be here for longer. He won't take me again. He doesn't do half-miracles.

But you know what women can be like when they won't let it go! Shauna just kept on at me until I finally agreed to have it done.

I was very quietly transferred to St Barts on April 12 for the operation with Professor Schilling, the man in charge of installing my so-called 'seatbelt'.

At St Barts there were a lot of African women working there and I soon became the flavour of the month. News soon got around that I was in for some treatment and one nurse came to me in my bed and said "we've all been praying for you" which was a lovely touch. But she then obviously went and told all her mates because before you knew it, one by one, every nurse in there seemed to walk through the doors to say hello!

However, news never leaked to the media that I had switched hospitals and that was for the best at the time. I didn't need any more attention, I just needed to go home.

The next day Professor Schilling popped up to see me and told me it would be alright and I had total faith. This man was the best in the world and even if I didn't truly want to have the operation, it was good to know I was being looked after so well. I spoke to dad and we prayed along with Shauna before I was then wheeled down for surgery. "Please, God, let's just get this over with," I said. "I want to get home as soon as possible."

I got into the theatre room and looked around and there were televisions on every wall, all ready to film what was about to happen. And as I lay there all I could think was 'I could nick one of those TVs and put it in my house – they are awesome'.

As you can tell, by this point I was beyond worrying. Cut me open, insert whatever is needed, sew me up, send me home. That is all I wanted to do.

I remember the needle and then I was gone. I don't really

remember coming around although I knew I felt as bad as ever. Groggy, confused, scared. I remember thinking 'I've been here before'.

Nobody knows this but during the operation I suffered another cardiac arrest. On this occasion though there was no need to panic, it was all part of the process.

In order to test the ICD, Professor Schilling and his team had to throw my heart out of line to check that the machine could throw me back in. It worked a treat.

All the evidence so far points to me being ok and I pray to God that I will never need the back up. However, I suppose it is nice for it to be in there, ready and able to deliver a shock if it's needed.

Yet I believe that God is still my only real saviour. He is the only one who can save me if I have a repeat episode. Yes the medical staff were great, yes everyone who has been involved in my recovery has been unbelievable.

But, ultimately, only God can help me.

The ICD is an incredible invention but if it is my time to die again then I can't argue with that.

I was finally discharged from hospital on April 16 – almost a month after my incident and to be able to walk outside freely and happily was a feeling I cannot describe.

A month in hospital is tough for anyone, especially someone used to being fit and strong, so to breathe fresh air along with Shauna was amazing.

I said goodbye to Dr Sam with a handshake and a smile. He had become a friend by then and he was the man who answered more questions than anyone else about my time inside. The rest of the doctors, nurses and everyone else who also kept an eye on me deserve just as much praise and respect and I know Dr Sam himself wants the praise spread fairly across all those who helped me walk out of St Barts alive and well.

It was time to go, it was time to get on with enjoying my family and friends. It was time to hear if all these rumours about my life turning upside down were true.

It was time to live.

#16

One Last Shot

ONE day when I was 10 me and my friends were looking for a game of football, just like we always used to do after school. We walked for miles until we ended up playing on a pitch inside an army camp. Camp Mobutu. Don't ask me why we thought that was a good idea.

On the camp there were not only soldiers but also their families. The sons of these soldiers were massive and had a tough mentality. They thought that just because their dads were in the army they were hard as well. We were playing on the pitch when some of these boys appeared. They told us to either leave the camp or take them on in a match.

We were out of our comfort zone. This wasn't our backyard and we felt a bit intimidated. I'm not ashamed to say I was really scared. I had a feeling that things could turn nasty.

But we agreed to play and I managed to stay out of trouble. No-body broke my leg, which was a bonus. I was playing at the back and after about 30 minutes I got the ball and ran through their team and scored. No-one will believe that but it's true!

It proved to be the winning goal. They couldn't get an equaliser no matter how hard they tried. In the end, well past what must have been the 90 minutes, they just drifted off, because they were exhausted. My goal had been the winner. I'll never forget it.

We were so happy but we still had to get off the camp in one piece. They weren't very happy with us. "Ok, we won so let's be cool," I said. We walked to the camp gates nice and slowly, our hearts beating big time until we got through – then we ran as fast as we could.

In Congo, if you go to another area and beat a team then you all sing on your way back to your town. You sing to make them angry and jealous, to let them know that they've been beaten, that although they may try and act tough, in reality they're not.

We legged it until we were miles away. And then we started singing one of the usual songs that is translated something like this: "We've come to your area and won. You might think you're a loud dog but you're nothing. Next time, come to our area and challenge us – we will beat you again." We were brave enough to sing – but only when we were miles away.

That was one of my earliest football triumphs. Going in to the lion's den and coming away as a winner. It felt so special.

I've been on quite a football journey, from the Congo to the Premier League. It wasn't easy in those early days. The bad pitches, no boots, the tougher older boys. When you've seen the rough then it makes you love the smooth. Grass, proper boots, a ball that doesn't wobble – kids in Europe have it easier than they will ever realise. If you want to know why so many African players are so strong physically and mentally in professional football, then look at what they came from, what they've battled against to get to where they are.

Next time you hear a kid moan because his boots aren't brand new or his mate has a better shirt or whatever, take them to one side and tell them how lucky they are to have anything on their feet at all.

#####

The main priority after coming out of hospital was enjoyment. When I was discharged we didn't return to Cheshire straight away because we knew the paparazzi were after us. That alone made my head spin. Why were they that bothered about me?

Instead of going home we went back to the apartment Shauna had rented in London and stayed there for a few days. It was just perfect. We had some time to ourselves, we ate at Wagamama every day, we were on the way back to normality. Never underestimate how good the simple things in life are.

We'd go for a walk every night at 11pm just to get out and to slowly build up my strength. I'd still be knackered in no time at all. Every night I'd try and reach a Tesco Express round the corner from the apartment before staggering back. I still had a lot of work to do, that much was clear.

After a few days Warwick got us a car to our place in Cheshire and getting back home was no different for me than it is anyone else. I was back in my own bed, I could chill on my own couch, nobody was watching me, monitoring me, I didn't have tubes and wires hanging out of my neck and nose and mouth and God knows where else. Making a cup of tea made me smile so much, watching the rain fall outside didn't bother me anymore, listening to Joshua sleeping – all these things, these tiny things made me almost cry with the joy of simply being here.

One of the guiltiest pleasures was getting my Blackberry back. I couldn't use it in hospital but I wasted no time catching up with all my mates and everyone who had sent good luck messages. I had a lot of people to thank. Loads of people visited the house and Ivan was the first guy to come round. He brought a big bottle of champagne to celebrate my life. We laughed and joked. It was just so amazing to be able to do what I wanted. Loads of the Bolton guys said hello, all my neighbours asked how I was and I couldn't go two minutes without a text from somebody telling me they were glad I was better.

During those first few days of 'freedom' the issue of the rest of my career refused to go away. How could it? I was a professional footballer who had died on the pitch. There were some serious questions to answer.

Football had been my life, my love. Something that had been with me throughout my early life in Congo and my new life in England. From winning at Camp Mobutu to holding my own at the highest level of the professional game. It had been a positive force through all the highs and lows.

As I started to try and adapt to normal life, so many memories came flooding back. Playing week in and week out in the Premier League gives you so many highs. Like playing at Old Trafford. What a place. I don't care what anyone says, it is tough playing there as one of the opposition. You feel like you're in a fight between 10 people and 200. The chances of winning are very small. I remember walking down the tunnel when I first played there for Birmingham in January 2008 and I was thinking 'Fabrice, boy, there is some serious stuff going on here'. It is a dream to be playing at such an arena.

I bent down and touched the grass. Here I was, a boy from Congo, about to play at Old Trafford. Amazing. I never thought for one day that this could happen.

The noise when they attacked was ridiculous – it was so annoying! You couldn't hear yourself think. For 10 minutes you're not your normal self. You look across at their side with the likes of Paul Scholes and Ryan Giggs and you want to ask for their autograph, never mind tackle them, although you soon click out of that and remember your job on the pitch.

I thought that I would love to step out at Old Trafford as a professional footballer again. Just once more. More memories kept flooding back. I even started thinking about the grounds I used to hate turning up at. How I would love to play there now.

Places like Goodison Park. I hated that place. When they go 1-0 up, you really feel you're going to lose. You just know it. I only won there once and couldn't wait to get out of there. The fans are right on top of you and the noise is amazing. Credit to those supporters, they know how to get their players to react. But as an opponent it's tough.

You also have to give credit to the Geordie people. St James' Park is like nothing on Earth. They know how to support their team well. They push their team forward. When I was at Birmingham, we beat them 5-1 in an FA Cup replay in January 2007 and I've never heard noise like it. You cannot shake the place off, the volume is incredible. When you walk on the pitch, you see the stand rising up to the sky and it takes you aback. Wow.

One of the best grounds to visit but the worst to play at by a long way. Their fans are mental – beyond mental!

Sunderland is another tough place to visit. When they score it's like they get another three players – the effect it has is ridiculous. I've run around their pitch thinking 'shut your mouth – just give me some quiet!'

Then there's Stoke City. Just mentioning the name makes me shiver. You don't ever want to play at the Britannia Stadium and especially not when Rory Delap is bombing those throw-ins at you. Oh my God. The first time we played Stoke, Gary Megson said: "For 20 minutes, let's do throw-ins." 20 minutes? More like 20 hours! We needed to work on protecting Jussi so he could come out and get the ball for us. We got into the game and Rory let one go. Wow. Is this guy for real?

I loved the different styles in the game. You'll hear no complaints from me about their footballing style, what a job Tony Pulis has done for them. But you will hear plenty of complaints about the Britannia. Cold, windy, noisy and chaotic. A Tuesday night game there is the stuff of nightmares. Everything seems to go for them there.

Playing at all these venues is why you play the game. It's hard not to be overwhelmed with nerves and excitement but you just have to do your best. Take a deep breath, feel like you belong and go from there.

When I first returned to Arsenal I was playing for Birmingham and it was a really strange sensation. I knew the game, just a week or so after playing at Old Trafford, was coming up – I'd searched for it early on when the fixtures came out – and I knew it would test my emotions.

I'd grown up at the club, they had pulled me out of a normal life and given me this amazing opportunity to provide for myself and my family financially while living the dream of being a footballer.

I knew I had to leave and I've never regretted that decision but going back there was always going to be a tough test. I knew every member of their starting XI that night – you can't tell me that doesn't have an emotional impact on you. It was different, I tried my best to concentrate but to play against the likes of Cesc Fabregas was always going to be hard. Arsenal were the club I had always wanted to play for. That was the dream. It didn't work out and that is life. I was determined to show the club that I was a good player, a player they should've kept.

As I stood in the tunnel at the Emirates preparing to go out, I remember thinking that here I was, once again, facing a trial at Arsenal. All those years ago Steve Leonard had told me to give it everything I had to try and impress and I had plans to do exactly the same again today – but this time against Arsenal instead of for them. It felt like I was being tested and that I had to make people sit up and realise the player and man I had become.

I was proud of my performance that day and felt I played well as we managed to get a 1-1 draw. Emmanuel Adebayor gave Arsenal the lead with a penalty before Garry O'Connor equalised for us and we were well happy with a point. To get a result made the day even better. The scrawny kid who had dreams of running out at the Emirates every week was now a Premier League player for Birmingham City – and loving every minute of it.

Of all the academy players taken on with me at Arsenal, I was the only one who managed to play in the Premier League. It just shows the level of dedication you need and the kind of person I am. If I was bad at something I HAD to work on it. I'd pushed myself to the limits to make my football dream come true.

I've still got my first Arsenal shirt, it's in the garage somewhere in a box, and I will get around to framing it one day. There is no doubt the club is in my heart – but that doesn't mean I didn't want to beat them every time I faced them for Birmingham or Bolton.

It's not the only shirt I have. Vieira sent me a signed one for my 21st birthday. I never got the chance to play against him, which is a massive regret, but when he was at Inter Milan a parcel arrived one day that blew me away. 'Happy birthday, my friend,' the message on the shirt read. 'Have a good day and enjoy yourself.' That shows you the class of the man. I would love to have played against him – but you will have to ask other people whether they would've been able to tell the difference between us…

I'd met so many good people, experienced so much camaraderie. It saddened me to think that I'd never share in the dressing room banter again. All these emotions and memories were swirling around inside me at the time.

#####

Professor Schilling had already spoken to me about my professional career. It was during my recovery, when getting better was the only thing on my mind, never mind playing football again.

He came into my hospital room to see me, along with Shauna and Dr Sam, and was as honest and as straight as can be.

"I'm sorry to tell you this but I advise you to retire," he said. "The tests we have taken show that you're heart is improving but you will never be able to put yourself through the stress needed to play professional football."

I didn't cry and neither was I surprised but after being discharged I had more time to think about it.

Was it really the end? Was it really all over?

One day I went to Euxton and it all hit home. I still had a key so I let myself in and went straight to my spot in the changing room. There was my locker. Right in front of me, my name in big letters:

FABRICE MUAMBA

I was stood in a deserted training room, the only noise being a tap dripping somewhere, and I prayed to God.

'Please God, let me get back to do this every single day. I want this routine, I want this routine back.'

I opened the locker and it was empty apart from some mail. Nothing else. No kit or boots which I was pleased about because I didn't want to cry, I didn't want more of a reminder of what I was missing.

For a second the thought of a future without football terrified me. I knew Dr Schilling was right but I had to be 100 per cent sure before I called it a day.

Perhaps there was a tiny glimmer of hope. Perhaps I would play again after all. I had to find out for sure.

#17

Blessed

I SUPPOSE I knew deep down that my career was over because guys like Professor Schilling don't make mistakes and on April 25 me, Shauna and Dr Tobin went down to St Barts to be told that officially.

Again, Professor Schilling hit me with it nice and clearly and told me that I could never play football. There were no half-answers or half-queries. It was over.

That should have been good enough for me. But it wasn't. What if there was a tiny, tiny chance I could fight against the odds again and return? I decided to head for a second opinion.

It was a decision that had absolutely nothing against those in London who had saved my life.

Professor Schilling is a man I have nothing but the highest

respect for but I just needed another voice, another person telling me it was useless. It was nothing personal. When you've done nothing but love playing football for as long as I have, then it felt right to get more advice.

So, on April 28, I travelled to Belgium with Dr Tobin to see Dr Pedro Brugada, a man with plenty of experience in treating what I'd been through.

Dr Brugada had fitted Belgium Under-23 international Anthony Van Loo with an ICD in 2008 and he had managed to start playing again. The ICD even kicked in one day when he collapsed as he was playing for SV Roeselare. Go and watch it on YouTube. The ICD jolts him back to life and he sits up straight away. I couldn't help but think maybe I could get the same sort of treatment, be given the same sort of chance.

All my notes were taken over to Belgium so Dr Brugada had all the information he needed. I had loads of tests as they tried to stimulate my heart to see how it would react. And when they did that they found a new problem. Basically, the electrical flow of your heart goes down certain channels which start at the top and move towards the bottom and branch out. But my electrical signals weren't quite following the right path, so a small operation was planned to fix that.

It was nothing to really worry about but maybe it was a sign that it really didn't look good as far as resuming my career was concerned. However, Dr Brugada wouldn't tell me on the day if it was all over, so I returned home with some small hope that I might be able to return. Dr Brugada wanted me to come back for a second opinion later in the year, even if Shauna and Dr Tobin believed it was not going to change anything. But hope can make your brain play tricks on you and I wouldn't give up on the idea of playing again. However, that was soon dashed in the second meeting. I returned to Belgium with Shauna and Dr Tobin for the small procedure needed to fix my pathway problem and also a final yes or no on my future.

Before I got the bad news, Dr Brugada and his team tried to identify the pathway problem with my heart but it had somehow cleared itself up. They stimulated my heart to try and find it but in the end they gave up. So what should have been a minor operation turned into a minor nothing.

More heart tests were done and I was kept in overnight. I woke up wondering what the day would bring. Even though my test results were better and my heart was strengthening itself, you don't go through what I went through without paying a price.

And, as expected, that price was my career.

It was a no.

It was always a no. I just needed to hear it again.

As it turns out, Professor Schilling's initial view that my heart didn't have the strength to cope with playing football was absolutely spot on.

In Dr Brugada's office he talked me through it step-by-step and explained why I no longer needed the small operation. But he then came out with it straight to leave me in absolutely no doubt. "You won't ever be able to play football again," he said.

"It's not just the risk of you having another cardiac arrest, your heart suffered so much damage in those 78 minutes that it cannot ever function at the level needed to play football."

I asked a few questions but I heard nothing I didn't expect or didn't know already. Dr Brugada and Dr Tobin left the room. Dr Tobin had to get back for Bolton's friendly with Barcelona 'B' that night, and I was ok with it. What can you do? I tried to be upbeat and ok. It was better to know, once and for all, what my future did and didn't contain.

Before leaving the room, Dr Brugada shook my hand and Shauna and I prayed. We then caught a flight home and got on with the rest of our lives.

#####

On that flight, I was able to think back about the good times in professional football that I'd experienced. I'd come up against so many great players. Some of them deserve a mention now.

Who is the greatest player I've ever seen? Paul Scholes. End of story. You know how some people have sat navs in their car? Paul Scholes has a sat nav in his head and it's tuned in to Old Trafford. He is just a hero, unbelievable. He is two minutes ahead of you.

You can ask any Premier League player and they will all tell you that he is head and shoulders above the rest. All you can do is respect the guy. He doesn't speak much anyway, never mind on the pitch, so you can't even wind him up or try and put him off. He knows what he wants to do with the ball before he's even got it.

I remember trying to tackle him once and he was gone, past me and away, before my brain had even clicked into gear. What a privilege it has been to face a man like that. And the best thing is that you can feel yourself learning when you're facing him.

His team-mate Ryan Giggs is another who I just love as a player. When he is running straight at you all you are thinking is 'I want to go home!' – he is that good. This guy is so far ahead of you and so clued up that you're helpless. He might be a skinny guy and you think 'I'll smash him' but you need to get near him first. And most of the time you can't lay a finger on him.

Although Scholes and Giggs don't say much on the field that can't be said of everyone in football. Craig Bellamy is the best for dishing out the verbals. He is an amazing footballer but he seems to need anger to drive him forward. Some players can only motivate themselves when they are fuming and Craig is one of them. I've played against him once or twice and I've heard him calling the referees some outrageous things! He is a really, really nice guy when he doesn't have his boots on but when he is on the pitch he is Mr Angry, and a very good player. He demands nothing but the best from his team-mates. He stands up for whatever team he plays for – he never hides and doesn't take crap from anybody.

Steven Gerrard is another leader. He is so quick and such a great athlete, he is like a horse. When he takes off, oh my God... When he performs there is nobody who can touch him. He can ping the ball serious distances. And I mean really ping the ball. When we played at Anfield on Boxing Day, 2008, Gary Megson made me try and man-mark Gerrard. What? Who does that? I was fit enough for the job and tried to stay with him but he was just too good. When he took off I thought 'Oh, Jesus!' and I just had to do my best. Everywhere he went, I went. I was his shadow.

And how did it go? Not very well, let's put it like that.

He started in midfield but then went up front so I followed him there. That then meant we had five at the back which opened up space in midfield for Xabi Alonso to do what he wanted. Gerrard knew exactly what he was doing; he is a very smart, very clever player.

Footballers sometimes don't get the credit they deserve for intelligence they've got out on the pitch. It takes a different kind of clever when that whistle blows. Players like Gerrard can run a game and smell trouble a mile off. I don't know him as a person but as a footballer the vibe you get is that he is very dedicated and driven. He wants to do nothing but win medals for Liverpool – I respect his loyalty and commitment.

Another player I used to always know I was in a game with is Lee Cattermole at Sunderland. That boy loves a tackle. He loves getting stuck in – bang, bang, bang! He was born that way and really enjoys it, which is just how it should be.

Then there is Didier Drogba. He is unplayable. On my very first game in the Premier League, when we lost at Stamford Bridge, Steve Bruce put a teamsheet up before the game and invited me to look at it. There's my name and I'm down to mark Didier Drogba at corners. He was on the bench that day but I was still terrified. I thought to myself 'is Steve on drugs?' He just grinned, knew what I was thinking and said: "Yeah, that's your job today." I thought he'd gone crazy!

On his day Didier really has the wow factor, just like Claude Makelele, Michael Ballack and Michael Essien. Chelsea have had so many amazing midfielders over the past few years. After playing them you just go home and try to work out how to improve and be better next time. After I first played against Ballack, I went home thinking 'how can he be that good?' It makes you realise just how tough football is.

Essien is an all-round footballer and an absolute powerhouse. About as complete a player as you can be. He can tackle, run, and do the lot. When you are in the Premier League you're there on merit and you just have to try your best. He was playing in my first Premier League match, too, so not only did I have Drogba to deal with but I had Essien powering past me.

Makelele was another 'machine' and a guy who took the holding midfield role to another level. When we played Chelsea at home that season I was speaking in French on the pitch when we were defending a corner. It's as noisy as anything and we're all trying to get organised when before you know it Makelele looks at me and, speaking in French, goes: "Where are you from?" I told him I was from Congo and he was delighted. "Are you really? As in Kinshasa, Congo? Wow, it's nice to meet you!" All this is going on as the chaos of the Premier League unfolded around us.

After the game I was getting changed when I was summoned into the Chelsea dressing room. One of their backroom staff came in and said "Claude wants a word." Uh-oh, I've been summoned. I walked into their dressing room and sat next to him – me in my shirt, him in his playing shorts and nothing else.

"Nice to meet you properly," he said. He then gave me his playing shirt and plenty of advice about life at the very top. It was a nice touch from a good man.

"You try really hard," he said.

"Thanks," I replied. "I've got no choice but to."

We shared a few laughs and jokes and it was a good experience. I was very humbled to see a man from the Congo who had gone that far. One day that could be me, or so I hoped.

So many great memories, so many great players.

#####

When I was in hospital recovering, I had a crazy dream. There is a Tesco Express in Wilmslow, near my house, and I dreamt that I strolled in there, without a care in the world, and filled in a Lotto ticket nice and slowly.

I returned home, turned the TV on and watched as my numbers rolled in one by one. To the tune of £150m – and I still remember the numbers! I can't tell you what they are but when I win it one day I will prove that the dream was for real. I've got those six lucky numbers written down in a secret place. Let's wait and see what happens.

I also told Shauna I'd won big.

"Shut up," she said. "What drugs are they giving you in here?" She asked me what the numbers were.

"You must be joking!" I replied. "Nobody finds out what they are. I'll win it and then I'll share it with you!"

Some people might think I've used up a lifetime's worth of luck already but I personally don't believe in the word 'luck'. It's not part of my vocabulary. There is no such word. The word I prefer is 'blessed'. Because that's how I feel.

I'll be honest – not going into training, not hearing the chat in the dressing room or running out to play at the weekend does still feel strange and frustrating from time to time but it's just a case of readjusting and refocusing on what matters.

I know I could go up to Bolton's training ground all day every day if I wanted to and the boys would make me as welcome as can be. But I'm not a player anymore so that's not for me. I owe Bolton everything but I can't be getting in the way while the boys train or anything like that. I have to move my focus on and do other things.

When I do get those twinges of regret about having to give up football I simply look at Shauna or Josh, or both of them, and remember that I'm breathing.

There's no need to cry about my retirement. As long as I can breathe and walk, what more do I want to be able to do? God is with me and that's what counts. I have an inner strength that helps me to deal with disappointments in life. That strength comes from my faith.

From a very young age, my mum took us to a Christian church not far from my house. It was a Pentecostal church. It was a must for the family, we just had to go and I grew up in a Christian house that was very respectful of God. I prayed every night with mum and dad. We prayed for strength and safety and a peaceful life. Christianity for me is the biggest factor in my life in every way you can think of.

Christmas in Congo is very different to life in England. There we celebrate the birth of Christ and it is like a big party, everybody has fun, the whole street gets together for a big feast. Chicken, rice, peas, plantain, you name it, and Christ is the centre of all the attention. In England it's not quite the same, people aren't as religious and that's absolutely fine. Every country is different and you have to respect each other's different ways and customs.

It's the same with New Year. In Congo, almost everyone spends New Year's Eve in church because they want to start the new year praising God. In the UK most people spend it in the pub! Different people, different attitudes. I personally go to church on New Year's Eve with the family to pray that next year will be better than this year and that what stopped me this year won't stop me over the next 12 months.

My faith in God gives me inner peace, I serve him and he's the person who can provide all my needs and wishes. I pray to a God who will never change; he will always be powerful, awesome and a guide to my life. He is the driver of my car – I'm just the passenger. When dad left we relied on God even more to keep him safe where he was and us safe where we were. The fact we all survived all the killings and trouble in the Congo proved that He was listening and answered our prayers.

I enjoyed being a footballer. I loved it in fact. But life goes on. I was past that. I am past that. We put a statement out in August after my second meeting with Dr Brugada and all I could do was thank everybody for their support. I didn't want anyone being upset.

Football lasts 90 minutes but my family lasts all day, every day. I'm the luckiest guy I know. Apart from anything, I've not had time to get too upset because life has gone absolutely crazy.

So crazy that you just would not believe it...

#18

All Together Now

I WAS in hospital from March 17 to April 16 and in the space
of a month my life became unrecognisable. I used to get spotted
every now and again because I was a footballer but this? This was
something completely off the scale.

The reaction to it all was so overwhelming and bigger than anything I could ever have imagined. In hospital I'd only picked up a
tiny bit of what was going on outside the four walls of my room.

Shauna would laugh and tell me that the world had changed
and Rashid would also come in and let me know that, overnight,
my story had become the biggest one out there.

"Fab," Rashid would say. "You've become massive. You're
trending on Twitter!"

I didn't have a clue what he was on about and I wasn't allowed my phone so I couldn't get any real access to the outside world. So there I am lying in a hospital bed, apparently at the centre of the biggest sports story in years, and I had no idea whatsoever.

My comedian friend Eddie Kadi came in to see me one day, sat on the edge of my bed and told me that everyone was going crazy for Fabrice. What? I was just a regular Premier League player one minute and now all this had happened. It was a lot to take. It wasn't until I picked up my phone afterwards and started scrolling through my messages that I got a sense of how massive this had become. 250 texts, 250 emails. Wow! All these people trying to ask me how I was and whether there was anything I needed.

It took me about two hours to go through everything and see how many good luck messages I had, how many prayers had been said in my name and also how many new Twitter followers I had! Wow! My life had exploded onto centre stage and I wasn't around to see it. I remember sitting with Shauna at home, trying to get my head around it, and she just grinned and said "I told you so." She wasn't wrong.

About a week after being released from hospital we decided to go and watch a late film at the cinema inside the Trafford Centre. Until then, I'd not really been out much, so I had no idea what the public really thought of me.

Me and Shauna were walking hand in hand through the Trafford Centre, minding our own business, when all of a sudden this huge bear of a man I didn't know came up and hugged me, completely out of the blue.

He just arrived from nowhere and tried to pick me up, squeezing me tight and shouting: "I'm so glad you're ok mate, I'm so glad." It was so strange but such a lovely moment. Shauna just stood next to me and said "didn't I tell you? Life is different now."

There have been plenty of moments like that and each and every one of them is a joy, even if it can be a bit frightening when people just walk up to you and hug you!

The response from the footballing world has also reduced me to tears at times and I cannot thank people enough for taking the time to wish me well.

When Bolton played Blackburn at the Reebok in the first game after my collapse the fans in the Nat Lofthouse Stand made the mosaic 'MUAMBA 6' out of cards they were holding and both sets of players wore 'MUAMBA 6' training shirts before the game. How can you not be moved and humbled by that? I was still in hospital at the time as it was only a week after the incident and I didn't really have much of clue what was going on.

Looking back on it now just makes me so thankful and proud. How can you look at the way the football world responded and not think it is the greatest sport in the world? Unfortunately for me, it took a cardiac arrest to underline how special football can be but it has all been worth it.

All over the world the game united to show how big its heart is. My old team-mate Gary Cahill was one of the first, wearing a 'Pray 4 Muamba' t-shirt under his Chelsea kit while the likes of Barcelona, Real Madrid and Arsenal also wore shirts with my name on them.

When it really mattered the worldwide football family pulled together like no other, and I will never be able to thank everyone for their support.

I wish I could go to every single club that supported me and shake the hands of the managers, players and chairmen who showed that much generosity.

There have been a few amazing moments that stand out. One

is when I went back to the Reebok for the match between Bolton and Spurs and the second time was when 'The Special One' Jose Mourinho, stopped me in a corridor to tell me he'd been praying for me. Can you imagine that? It is moments like this which sum up how random my life has become.

It happened like this. Shauna, Joshua and me were in Jamaica in early June, catching some sun and slowly chilling out and recuperating. It was a break we all needed but it was about to end in the greatest way possible.

I was lying on the beach messing around with Joshua, thinking just how great it was to be alive and well, when Shauna told me to pack my bags. "What?" I said.

"You need to catch a flight to Spain," she said. "Real Madrid have been in touch. I've just had an email and they want you to kick off a game on Sunday between Real Madrid legends and Manchester United legends."

"Whatever, Shauna," I replied, not sure about what she was really saying. "Which legends?"

"I don't know," she said. "Some guy called Zidane is playing."

Ha ha, this was the best joke ever. "So, Shauna, you're trying to tell me that Real Madrid want to fly me all the way from Jamaica to Spain just to start a charity game?"

"Yes," she said. "That's exactly what I'm saying."

I swore! And then I saw the list of people playing and I swore even more! Wow! Two sides full of complete and utter greats.

I was just so stunned. This was the Friday so I had to move fast. I threw some stuff in a case, caught a flight from Jamaica to Miami and then Miami to Madrid. By the time I got back to Europe it was the early hours of Sunday morning so I went straight to bed to try and shrug off any jetlag.

I walked down to reception after my sleep and I bumped straight into a host of United legends. Bryan Robson, Teddy Sheringham, Dwight Yorke and Andy Cole. I'd already been in touch with Coley to tell him I'd be in Madrid that night and it was great to catch up with him.

Everyone was great with me. Andy shook my hand and introduced me to all the other guys. It was a wonderful life experience. They all asked me how my health was, how the family was and what my plans were for the future. I felt so pleased and humbled to be in the presence of such guys. My playing career might have ended but would I have had moments like this if I hadn't collapsed? I doubted it then and I doubt it now.

The hotel we stayed at was only two minutes from the Santiago Bernabeu so we got to the ground very early and I got the full stadium tour before being taken to meet the club president Florentino Perez in his super-VIP suite. He took me by the arm, shook my hand and told me to stay strong. He knew how I was feeling because his wife Pitina had died of a heart attack just before my visit.

"I know what you're going through" he said, his voice as steady as a rock. "My thoughts and prayers are with you and your family."

That was an incredible moment from a man in mourning and a glimpse behind the scenes and a glimpse at the decency of people in the game.

As I walked out of the suite to prepare for my kick-off duties, the day got even more surreal when Mourinho bumped into me as I headed to see where my seat was. He was walking past me and said: "Fabrice?"

I was amazed he even knew who I was!

He looked as slick as always in a suit and tie and shook my hand.

"How are you?" he said. "It's so great to see you. You had us all praying hard for you."

"It's nice to see you, too, Mr Mourinho," I replied, pretty sure I was now in some sort of dream.

"I hope everything is ok for you from now on," he said. "If you ever want to come to Madrid to watch us then you are welcome to come any time you want."

He shook my hand again and left. That was another lovely gesture in a day full of them. Two hours before the match I was taken downstairs into the bottom of the stadium to meet the players from both teams. A club official took me down in a lift and I was so nervous. I was getting the chance of a lifetime. I might have been a professional footballer but don't forget I'm a fan first. Any person offered that chance should be very excited. When the lift pinged open I walked down and turned to my left and then turned left again into the Real Madrid dressing room.

"Fabrice?" someone shouted from the far side of the room. I turned around and there is Zinedine Zidane, already in his matchday kit, shouting "Fabrice, come over here."

What was going on? Zidane knows my name? He didn't know it before I died but he does now. Who cares how or why he knows it – Zidane knows my name! He started talking to me in French, shaking my hand and asking how I was feeling.

"You're a very blessed guy," he said. He wasn't lying either.

Fernando Hierro then came over and he was also great with me, asking about my treatment and the family. I could barely take it all in. The dressing rooms alone were unbelievable, never mind the players sat inside them.

As I'm standing around admiring all the players and trying to absorb the fact that Zidane knows who I am, Luis Figo walks through the door of the changing room, takes one look at me, clicks his fingers and goes "Ah, Fab."

I'm not even Fabrice to this guy, I'm Fab! It's like we're mates! This is getting ridiculous. From the Congo to being a mate of Zidane and Figo.

What a ride.

Did Figo – *the* Figo – just call me 'Fab?' Eh?

"How are you, my friend?" he said.

"I'm cool, my friend," I replied, laughing out loud. What a story. That room probably had about half a billion pounds worth of talent in it. Zidane, Figo, Hierro, Fernando Morientes, Fernando Redondo, Roberto Carlos, I could go on and on and on. It was ridiculous. All the top Madrid heroes – plus me!

I left the Real dressing room just before the game was about to begin. The players went out first as I waited behind in the tunnel. I was feeling so nervous but really excited until, finally, the stadium announcer mentioned that I was there and summoned me onto the pitch.

What do you say about the Bernabeu? It is unbelievable. The noise, the height of the stands, the passion and intensity – and this was just a charity game. 80,000 people rose, cheered and clapped when I walked out. It was one of the most emotional moments of my life.

The referee was the Italian Pierluigi Collina – you know it's a big game when even the ref is a legend – and he shook my hand, whispered "good luck for the future" into my ear and then invited me to kick off. By this point I was working so hard to keep the tears in. I put the ball on the spot and passed to Zidane.

That means I can say I played with the great man himself. A

truly priceless moment. I got the lift back up to my match seat and I couldn't find the words to express how I felt or how thankful I was to get the opportunity.

#####

The fans of Bolton and Spurs had already given me one night to remember in early May when I went back to the Reebok Stadium for the first time. I'd wanted to go for a while to watch a game and that seemed like the best one to pick because of the two teams involved. I was a special guest of Mr Gartside and the club and I was nervous about what would happen but the reception I got from all the fans at the ground when I arrived soon put me at ease. What can I say? What do you say? I'm lost for words when it comes to trying to express my happiness and love for those who cared for me and those who cried for me – whether they are Bolton fans or not. That night I got out of the car at the front of the stadium and fans were clapping and cheering from the moment I was spotted.

Nobody had done that at Bolton when I was on the pitch!

Dean, the player liaison officer, greeted me at the front door. "Good to see you, little man," I said with a grin. "And you," he replied. It was like I'd never been away.

I went to see Owen and we spoke for a while, both of us grinning big time. He said I could go in and see the boys in the dressing room. It was great to walk in there. Everyone shook my hand and after doing a television interview I met Harry Redknapp as well. "How are you doing?" he asked. "You scared us a bit. It's great to see you doing so well." I also met Dr Mughal and Geoff Scott, the two medical guys from Spurs who ran on. How do you thank people for saving your life? What can you say or give or do to repay them? It was overwhelming and a humbling experience to meet those guys.

Tears were never far from the surface and I couldn't hold on any more when I walked on to the pitch. Man, the Reebok was rocking that day! The noise was incredible, fans from both sides were clapping and chanting. I applauded all four corners of the ground and tried to hold it together but it was so tough. I will never forget that day, that moment. I came off the pitch and Neil McLeod, my PR agent, and Phil, the club chaplain, took me into a quiet side room and gave me a hug and a chance to catch my breath and try and absorb what had just happened. How often can you say that every single football fan in one ground is delighted to see you there? That is what it was like that day. You could feel the emotion and the special atmosphere. I love winning more than anyone you will ever meet but there are bigger and better things to worry about and those fans that day proved that. It made me cry then and it can make me emotional now.

No thanks will ever be enough.

Another great experience was the Football Writers' Association awards in London the day after the match. Matt Dickinson from *The Times* got in touch and invited me along. It was one of the best decisions I've ever made.

Me and Shauna travelled to London and the day was unbelievable from start to finish. First of all, a woman came up to me in the street and started holding my face in the palms of her hands. "I just want to touch you, I just want to touch you," she said. She was one of thousands who've shaken my hand, hugged me, asked for a photo or a smile.

"I want to touch the miracle," she continued. I've gone from wearing the number six shirt for Bolton to becoming a 'miracle' have I? Wow. I couldn't get used to all this attention.

We then went in to Selfridges to buy Shauna a dress for the event that night and as I passed my card over the counter, the guy took two looks at my name and went "it's you!"

Next thing we know we're being swept upstairs into a private suite where we were offered champagne and canapés. Nothing was too much. Everybody just wanted to smile and say hi and shake my hand.

Nobody had to do that for us. Selfridges didn't ask or want anything in return. It was just another example of how amazing people really are. There have been so many other instances that show how much people care. And I mean that.

At the awards that night I kept nice and low key until they announced that I was there so I stood up and waved. There was a real genuine gasp from everywhere in the room before Robin van Persie came down from the top table and gave me a hug.

"Great to see you," he whispered. "We're all so pleased you're ok." There I am, in a room full of journalists and I couldn't hear myself think. There were laughs and cheers and tears being shed by more than a few people and I wasn't far behind. Afterwards I shook a million hands and heard a million stories about who was where when I collapsed, what they thought, how they felt. I got nothing but positive vibes from everyone and as I looked around the room I thought to myself: 'My God. I'm not the Fabrice I was a month ago.'

There have been so many memories already. For example, I was meeting Warwick one day in London and had to get a cab from Euston to Warwick's offices. All of a sudden the taxi driver started talking about people who had died suddenly and I told him that it had happened to me.

"What?" he said. "Yeah, it happened to me. I had a cardiac arrest but managed to survive." "Are you that Muamba guy?" he asked and when I told him I was he went crazy. He slammed the brakes on and went: "Really? Wow. Listen mate, I'll take you for free now. You're one hell of a fighter so don't worry about paying." He was a proper Cockney guy with a big smile and he wouldn't shut up once he found out it was me. He told me he wanted a picture and that his kids wouldn't believe him. I kept trying to pay him but he wouldn't listen. I was so overwhelmed by his response. What can you do but say thank you? We pulled up and he jumped out and we had a picture before he hugged me. Incredible.

Loads of little things have changed – even going to Tesco. I used to go and mind my own business but the first time I went in afterwards somebody recognised me and before we knew it the manager came over and told us how great it was to meet me and that if I needed any help then to shout up.

Then, in June, me and my mates went out in London one night to a club called Bond. We just wanted a good laugh and to catch up and relax. Everything was chilled out and we were having a quiet night until I was spotted. "Are you Fabrice?" someone asked. "Yes, I am," I said.

All of a sudden everybody was at our table, trying to buy us drinks, taking pictures and hugging me. I wasn't drinking so I was turning down all these kind offers but it was so great and so nice to see this response from complete strangers. Some were saying that they had been praying for me. What can you say to that? Wow. It's just been a great journey.

At the end of the season, me and Shauna also went to the FA

Cup final between Liverpool and Chelsea. We sat in the corporate section where I was introduced to the crowd so I had to stand up and wave. About five seconds later, Gerard Houllier, the former Liverpool and Aston Villa manager who has also had heart trouble, came over to speak to me. We spoke in French and compared medical problems and had a joke. "When you have time, come to France and we can catch up," he said. "Take care."

Liverpool owner John Henry also said hello. He was great as well, praising me for fighting back and looking so healthy.

I couldn't stop grinning about being surrounded by all these people. I suppose even millionaires and important people are still human beings underneath it all and want to see others being happy and healthy.

Nothing negative has come from this. I think some idiot got into trouble on Twitter for wishing me dead or something like that but who is he? Who cares? I've got the whole country in my corner, I can cope with the odd loser here and there.

I've still got four massive boxes of letters and emails from people wishing me well. Phil Mason gave them to me and they're sat in my office. There are so many of them, including one amazing letter from kids in Ghana telling me they were praying for me. I've never even been to Ghana and a school wrote to let me know they wanted me to get better. That shows how many people were aware of my story and were praying for my recovery. I believe I'm a good person and I'm someone who has lived a good life. When you do that then good things head back in your direction.

I can't begin to describe all the cool stuff that has happened but I've got to mention the 'Britain's Got Talent' final I went to with Shauna. What a crazy night that was!

We got the invite and jumped at the chance. It was a night on the town in London and a chance to see yet another side of life. We booked a room in The Mayfair Hotel and when we checked in they told us they had upgraded us to a suite. Again, nobody asked for this. It was just the kind of generosity that has followed me about since everything happened. I felt so embarrassed about accepting the offer because I think you should always work for what you get in life but they insisted. We played it nice and cool as we walked up to this massive suite, we were shown around it and nodded respectfully. And then we closed the door and burst out laughing at it all. Wow. Life had become so random in no time at all. All this? For me? For real?

After the show I asked if I could meet Simon Cowell and one of his assistants told me "we'll do our best, he's a busy man." But eventually I was taken backstage and his dressing room door was open. "Fabrice!" he said, before shaking my hand. He invited me in and we spoke for a bit about my health and the future. I also met Pudsey, the dog that actually won the final. What do you say though? What can you say? It's a dog!

As a Congo boy who grew up in London, it was amazing to see what the Olympics did to change the place and the area I know well.

I was the same as everyone else over the summer and I couldn't stop buzzing about how incredible Team GB were and how the whole of London and the country united behind it. It was awesome and very humbling to be involved in a small way.

First of all, on July 20, I was asked to run with the Olympic torch through my home London borough of Waltham Forest.

The organisers got in touch with Neil and everyone thought it was a great idea – who would turn down a chance like that? I've still got the torch in the garage and I'm trying to find a frame to stick it in. It has become one of my proudest possessions and a reminder of how lucky I've become.

In early August, just as the Olympics were really firing, I also appeared on Piers Morgan's show on CNN. He was over from America for the Olympics and is a massive Arsenal fan. Aren't we all? We met in Bow and he was great – very friendly and very interested in what had happened. We spoke about Arsenal and Arsene and everything else and I also revealed that I'd been back on a football pitch since my collapse when I played in Dubai.

It happened when we went there to spend some time together as a family and get away from everything. I figured that if anyone deserved a holiday after what happened then I did. We stayed at the One&Only hotel and had a great time. We've been there about seven times. Joshua loves the weather and it's a great place for families.

I was hanging around the pool, sipping orange juice under an umbrella, when a lifeguard came over to me and told me there was a game of football going on around the other side of the hotel. "Shauna, I think I'm going to go and play football, you know," I said. "I feel fine and some other guys are playing." Shauna was dangling her feet in the pool, keeping an eye on Joshua and she didn't really know what to say. "Really? Ok then." I started walking around to the game and Joshua caught up with me – he wanted to see his daddy in action again.

Some other footballers were staying there. So I walked around to where the game was and Jordan Henderson, Kieran Richardson and Danny Graham were all playing a game against the hotel staff. I saw those guys and just knew I had to get involved. It just seemed the right thing to do. I didn't think it would kill me, I just wanted to feel a ball at my feet again.

What can I say? It was amazing. I walked on to the grass pitch barefooted – back to where I began – and I asked if I could play. All of a sudden the teams changed around a bit and I was on the same side as Jordan, Kieran and Danny. "Just take it easy," Jordan said. "If you want to play then great but if you need to relax or take it easy then do it. No pressure here mate, just enjoy it."

We were all laughing and smiling and just having a great time. The sun was shining, my family were ok and I was about to have a kickabout. Perfect.

Touching the ball again was incredible. I tackled one of their players and laid the ball off to Kieran. I couldn't stop grinning and laughing. It was a simple tackle but it was one of the best I ever made. 'Wow I've missed this,' I thought to myself. I was full of the feelgood factor.

I played for about 20 minutes and built up a real sweat. It just felt so good because I missed playing, I missed the adrenaline, the excitement, everything. Danny scored a tap-in as we won 1-0. I just kept it simple and played at the back. All the guests were taking pictures and I wasn't that bothered about it getting out that I'd been playing. It didn't matter who found out. I only played for a short time so it wasn't going to harm anyone, especially not me. I never worried – I'd already beaten my biggest fears so I just got on with it.

Joshua was loving it from the sidelines and kept shouting out but he wasn't as excited as I was that day. The guys were great with me and were constantly monitoring me and telling me to take it easy and do things at my own pace. I was grateful that they cared and showed it. I was more interested in forgetting everything that had happened and just getting on with passing and moving and winning.

Even though the time flew by, I paid the price the next morning. "Shauna," I said. "I can't move, I can't get out of bed."

Wow, the muscles in my back and legs were so sore and stiff. It was probably a sign that my body was still recovering. I chilled out in the pool that day – there was going to be no repeat performance, that's for sure.

#19

No Limits

ALL the experiences I have had since my collapse have made me really happy but, of course, I still know what is the most important thing in life. Just after I left hospital, there was one person I still needed to see. This would turn out to be the best visit of all. Mum. She flew over from Congo for a visit. I knew she was coming and paced the house, desperate to see her. I was looking through the windows at the street when I saw the car she was in arrive. I ran outside as she got out and we hugged.

"Fabrice, Fabrice," she said over and over again, patting my cheeks and touching my hair, thinking I'm five years old again.

"My son, I love you so much. My son, my son," she kept repeating, hardly believing I was alive. She wasn't the only one.

I had seen her in Dubai 18 months beforehand but everything

that had happened meant we were closer than ever. She had almost lost her only son. Again. You can work out exactly how happy she was to see me looking fit and well.

It seemed so long since I had looked back at her in the airport in floods of tears waving me goodbye. So much had happened. So much drama. It wouldn't be long before I would return to the exact same spot where I left my old life behind all those years ago. It was time to return to Africa.

I didn't tell the whole world I was going. I wanted to keep it nice and relaxed without too much hassle. I flew from Manchester to Paris then Paris to Kinshasa and I couldn't help thinking about the journey I made in the opposite direction when I was just a boy. I was nervous but also excited at the same time. England is my home but the thought of returning to Africa excited me. I left Congo as a boy and was going back as a man.

The plane cruised towards the airport terminal and I looked through the windows, trying to see what I could remember and what was different. Everything had changed! Construction sites everywhere. I recognised the place where I said goodbye to mum, I could never forget where that was, and everything came flooding back. The fear we lived in, the uncertain times, dad having to leave, me following years later – everything. It felt so strange but also exciting to be back.

Congo is an amazing country and its potential is unbelievable but only if the country pulls together. The people are so strong, determined and hard working. It is so rich in natural resources that it should be in the top one or two African countries but instead it is near the bottom. Somewhere down the line, something is going wrong. At least most of the killings have stopped, though it still can be a dangerous place to live.

I went back for 10 days. Mum picked me up and the first thing we did was travel to Pastor Claude's house, about 45 minutes from the airport. It was the first time I'd met him face to face. "I'm so glad you came to see me," he said. "You will see on Thursday what you mean to these people."

We spoke a lot and it was so humbling. We then travelled to mum's house. It is a different house to where I grew up and as we pulled up there were so many people outside.

"What are they doing here, mum?" I said.

"They're here to see you, Fabrice," she said. Wow. I couldn't even get out of the car. Aunties, uncles, nephews and nieces. You name it, there were people from all over the place, family and friends. People were crying and cuddling me, it was just so amazing. About 25 of us squeezed into mum's front room and we prayed before I got hit with a million questions. Mum is very quiet but the rest of my family aren't and we had an amazing afternoon.

She also invited some old friends around who hadn't heard I was back in the country. I hid in another room and when I heard my name being mentioned I walked out and said: "Which Fabrice are you talking about – this Fabrice?" They were all so shocked! It was great.

Shauna and Joshua also came with me and he loved it. He just played in the sand all day and everyone made a huge fuss of him. He was surrounded by other kids.

On the Thursday we went to church and again only a few people knew I was going to be there. Pastor Claude did a service and at the end mentioned I was present. "Remember the man we have been praying for," he said. "Now he is here to visit us. Please welcome Fabrice."

Oh my God. The noise was something else. Tears started running down my face and I had to say hello to everyone. It was so moving and so incredible to be there with them. There were so many people there, about 500, and they all wanted a hug. My arms felt like they would fall off in the end!

When the time came to leave I was sad. Who wouldn't be after a trip like that? But at least it was under happier circumstances than last time.

I've often tried to get mum to move over to England and be with us but she is more comfortable over there. She is on the go all the time and she feels safe and happy these days, which makes me want to cry with joy and relief. Finally, I can stop worrying.

So I said my goodbyes and caught a plane from Kinshasa again. This time, though, I wasn't flying into the unknown, facing an uncertain future and I knew I could see mum anytime I wanted to.

#####

People ask me all the time 'what now?' or 'how do you feel?' and although it is still early days, the only answer I can give is that I feel blessed. I'm too blessed to be stressed.

Close your eyes and count to five. Go on, do it. One... two... three... four... five...

How many breaths did you take during that time?

One? A couple? Maybe three?

Every single one of them is a victory. Every. Last. One.

It's a victory for you, for your family and for your loved ones. Because it means you're still alive and still able to live a good, interesting, caring life.

I thought most of these things anyway as I ran onto that White Hart Lane pitch that night. I wasn't thinking anything when I was carried off but what happened has just sharpened my belief that every second, every smile you see in the street and every child you see hugging their parent is a complete blessing.

At the moment I can breathe, I can play with my son and I can kiss Shauna. That means I'm winning and winning comfortably. I've come back from the dead – what isn't possible now? It has changed my life for the better. I've always been a family man but my time with Shauna and Joshua and mum and dad is now more precious than ever. I want to be surrounded by friends and family and enjoy what they give me.

When Joshua arrived he made me realise what matters. He is the greatest thing that has ever happened to me and being there for him was the most important thing I could do.

Shauna is caring, loving and has the biggest heart. She is my numero uno. You know how President Obama has Michelle as his First Lady? She is my First Lady – you can't beat that.

I'm so glad that a month or so before I had my cardiac arrest, I left her in no doubt about how I felt.

It was Valentine's Day and I had something special planned. Something I'd wanted to do for a while. I wanted to put a ring on her finger. My good friend Andy Cole recommended a good jeweller and I organised it all.

We caught the train to London, we stayed at the Sanderson Hotel and I made sure the room had candles and roses and all that romantic stuff.

At about 7.30pm, after a day walking around London shopping in places like Harrods and Selfridges, we got changed for dinner and the ring was in my top pocket.

"We've been together for a long time," I said. "And you've always been there for me. Will you marry me?"

"Are you for real?" she said.

"Definitely," I said.

"Well, where is the ring then?" she said.

I had forgotten to even get the ring out! I was that nervous it had totally slipped my mind! What an idiot.

We then laughed, I put the ring on and that was it – it's for life. We kissed, went out for dinner and the next thing I know she's put it on Twitter – and the world went crazy!

We went out to eat at the Hilton Hotel on Park Lane and it was amazing, the start of us being together forever. We finally got married just a couple of weeks ago, in front of family and friends. It was the perfect ending of one chapter of our lives and the perfect opening to another.

When I moved to Birmingham, I went from living in a God-filled home to not attending church at all. I paid the price for that for a short while and lost my way.

I've made up for that and every Sunday I go to the Audacious Church in Manchester where there is lots of singing, praying and Bible reading. I read the Bible every morning and night and as long as Christ is in me I can have victory and glory in any situation I come across.

Joshua will be brought up the same. It helped me to get better, it strengthened my faith and it means I don't carry any fear.

I'm convinced God was with me during my 'death'. For 78 minutes I was no longer here. I didn't see any angels or Jesus but I was gone. I can't tell you where I went – I was just gone.

It all happened for a reason. There is more to it than that. It is the phenomenon of how God works. Things happen that we don't understand. Dr Deaner, Dr Tobin, all of them, were there for a reason. It's all part of a plan that we cannot get our heads around. All the men and women who saved my life did an amazing job, an incredible job and they did it for a reason.

I would love it if what happened could be used as a shining example of just how amazing the health services are in the UK. The NHS is unbelievable – so good it takes my breath away. Paramedics, doctors, the guys who drive the ambulances, the nurses and everyone else deserve more credit and more thanks than I can ever express. They are the real heroes in society. They are the real heroes in my story too. They get brushed aside but they keep the country alive.

#####

I want there to be a positive impact from this story and for me to be an inspiration to other people and show them that you can do anything – anything – with your life if you're willing to go out there and get it. As far as you can see is as far as you can reach. Visualise something and do it. It's as simple as that.

I look at it in this light because I realise how much worse this could have been. A tiny decision made here or there, a split-second of bad luck, a faulty defibrillator machine – whatever – means you wouldn't be reading this book, I wouldn't be here, Joshua wouldn't have his dad.

What, then, is there not to be positive about? I have a second chance at life and I want to use that and be as positive as can be. I don't dwell on the end of my career – carrying any bitterness in my heart will not change anything.

Look at it like this: all footballers have to retire at some point. I just had to retire early, that's all. It's a great sport and has given me more than I could ever have imagined but I was always going to have to jump off the ride one day. In a perfect world that would be 15 years from now. But we don't live in a perfect world. I'm just happy to be alive in any world.

Having to retire doesn't mean I can't be a good dad, a good husband, a good son. As far as I'm concerned I've been born again; this is my second life, my second chance. Why would I be depressed or down about that?

I was by no means perfect before my collapse but it has shown me what I need to do to improve as a person. Maybe the way I spoke to Shauna at times, or the way I was around the house, wasn't as it should be but that is all over now. I'm more humble than ever. More thankful. More grateful.

Nowadays I appreciate the tiny things in life so much more. To be able to play with Joshua in the garden, to be able to see him swimming in the sea as me and Shauna watch and laugh at him, to listen to great music and eat interesting food. These are the things that make me smile.

You have no idea, unless you've been there, how much of a thrill it is simply to walk, to breathe with no wires sticking out of your body, to run upstairs to fetch your glasses, to nip to the shops, to pick the little man up from school – the lot.

If you have your health then you have everything and sometimes you have to go to the other side to appreciate what is on this side. You cannot buy that.

I want the people reading this book to know that every single situation has some good inside it somewhere. Yes, you may have to look, and look hard, but it is there. I've certainly found the good from my incident and want to use that to make the future even better. It's strengthened my belief in the idea that people have to look at themselves and Do Good. That may seem like an easy thing to say but I mean it and I want to help in any way I can.

Enjoy your life. If you're a parent be a good parent, be a good father to your children and be a good husband to your wife. By doing good – getting educated, loving your parents, getting a job – you are living a worthwhile life. If you're not doing those things then you're hurting yourself and everyone else around you.

When the riots kicked off in London in August 2011 I was so sad and so upset. Not just because I grew up in the city but because of how pointless it was. Why? Every action has a reaction and that wasn't the right one to what was going on in London and the country. So many kids don't realise how lucky they are to live in a country which offers them so many chances. I'm no politician and I haven't got all the answers but when I saw that I just felt so helpless. Some people need a wake-up call to understand how great England is and how much of a chance it gives you to make something of yourself.

Education is so big a deal and so important but some youngsters don't realise that and I'd love to help get that message across. Yes, dream of being a footballer or an actress but don't dream of being any of them before you realise and understand that education comes before and above everything else. That's what I owe my dad and I will never be able to fully thank him.

I would like to go into schools and prisons and tell people my story. Show them that if a boy from Congo can make it, die, come back and keep on making it then anyone can.

ABSOLUTELY ANYONE.

I would love to walk in to Oxford University one day and do the same. Stick me in a lecture hall in front of 200 people and tell them the deal. Tell them that there are no limits in life. Nope. No way. I'm limitless and so is everyone else. The only limits are the ones you place on yourself and the lack of vision you show.

If you don't even try and find out how far you can see, how far you can dream and how much you can achieve, then what is the point? If you don't want to see if your car has five gears then you'll always be stuck in first while everyone else races past you.

I want those reading this book to realise that you can do anything you want with your life if you work hard. Nothing is impossible.

I'm a young man with the energy and drive I always had – just not the same outlet for it. But that doesn't mean I can't find other directions and projects to spend my life on and I'm determined that my story will not be frittered away, will not be forgotten. Fabrice Muamba – the man who came back; that is a tale I want to tell again and again until my message comes across loud and clear.

I've been involved with the Arrhythmia Alliance and British Heart Foundation since my retirement, delivering a petition to Downing Street in order to get CPR taught so young people know how to do what is necessary to try and save somebody's life. So many people get struck down by cardiac arrest these days so more knowledge and publicity is needed.

People suffer what I did on a daily basis but, let's be brutally honest, most don't make it because nobody knows how to help them. The guy who collapses in the supermarket should have the same chance I had because those around him know what to do. Sadly at the moment that is not the case. I can help change all that though. As part of an ambassadorial role with Bolton I will take part in the 'Hearts and Goals' campaign which will raise more awareness about cardiac arrests as well as provide 500 defibrillator kits for communities across the country.

On a religious note I also think my story is interesting and inspirational. Some people have told me I should become a pastor! Maybe that's because I get so passionate when talking about God, maybe it's because my face is quite well known now, and maybe it's both. Who knows what's in store for me? I do believe that there is a God that heard everybody's prayers. It's mind-blowing how everybody stopped and said a quick prayer for me. When I came out of hospital I was told about the hundreds of thousands of people who wrote #PrayforMuamba on their Twitter accounts and it all helped – I have absolutely no doubts about that.

#####

If I ever want a reminder of how close I came to not being here I unfortunately don't have to think too hard to come up with examples. Just before I left hospital, Shauna pecked me on the head one morning and mentioned that she had to tell me something. She had been keeping some news back for a couple of days because she didn't know how to say it. "What is it?" I asked nervously.

"A player in Italy has died," she said. "A guy called Piermario Morosini who plays for Livorno has had a cardiac arrest. He didn't make it."

What do you say to that?

It really, really upset me. I had to take a moment for myself and think about that. I feel so sorry for his family and friends. A fortnight or so after Shauna mentioned that, Alexander Dale Oen, one of Norway's best swimmers, suffered a cardiac arrest in the shower after training and also died.

Two young men, just as fit as me, just as happy as me, just as ready to take on the world as me.

They died and I didn't. What do you say to that?

People went: "That could've been you" and I shook my head and said "that WAS me."

Maybe that helps you understand why every single day is now a huge blessing. May they both Rest In Peace.

I suppose in one sense it is inevitable that my life would change and become more public after what happened but I'm sure I will remain the same ordinary dude. A few offers have come in to go on different television shows but I still don't really think of myself as a celebrity even if I'm very flattered by all the attention. I'm just an ordinary dude who's experienced something out of the ordinary. When I hear about all these new offers, these new angles I just laugh – I'm just me, the same old Fabrice.

I like my everyday life, thank you very much. I don't want that to be disrupted. I take Joshua to school, have some breakfast, read, sort paperwork out, do whatever needs doing and keep my head down. Why do I need that to change?

The physical effects of my collapse obviously mean that playing football is a no-no but I still love the game as much as I always did. Family first, football second. It was always that way anyhow but even more so now.

I've been told I can start light exercise such as swimming and some gym work, which is a relief, and it will be great to try and build up a sweat again. Apart from the odd memory problem here and there I'm in perfect condition and I look pretty much the same as I did during my playing career. My heart has been fine since my collapse, apart from a tiny correction it made when I was in France in the summer. It's comforting to know the ICD is fine and works and it was nothing to really worry about. I feel great at the moment thanks to my family, my friends, the medical staff who looked after me and God.

Add those together and nothing is going to hold me back.

So do I have any regrets? I suppose that's the biggest question of the lot.

And the answer is no.

It happened. I couldn't control it, this is what miracles are made of. Did you know that no doctor can put an exact finger on exactly what went wrong and then what went right? You cannot explain that. It's just part of the bigger picture and you have to move forward. I'm 100 per cent sure that if God wanted me to die I would've done so on that pitch. Why wouldn't I have done? Think about it. Who comes back from that? But my survival has convinced me there is a reason for it all – even if I'm still trying to work that reason out.

Only the future can tell me. Only the future will make that clear. At the moment, the fact I've got any future at all is enough to make me smile.

I've done enough dying to last a lifetime.

Index